P9-BIT-136

SGI President Ikeda
greets friends from around the world.

# FOR TODAY
### &
# TOMORROW
*Daily Encouragement*

# FOR TODAY
## &
# TOMORROW

*Daily Encouragement*

# DAISAKU IKEDA

World Tribune Press

Published by World Tribune Press,
606 Wilshire Blvd., Santa Monica, CA 90401.

Copyright © 1999, 2006 by Soka Gakkai

ISBN: 978-0-915678-63-1

*Design and illustrations by Alma Orenstein*

20 19 18 17 16 15 14 13

# PREFACE

PEOPLE OFTEN HAVE A PHRASE OR MOTTO that sees them through difficult or important times. A short saying, a few words, can determine the course of one's entire life.

As we seek a path to peace and happiness based on the principles of Buddhism while struggling with life's stern realities, having a guideline by which to live positively is of immeasurable value.

As Nichiren Daishonin writes, "To teach another something is . . . like floating a boat upon the water so that it may move ahead without difficulty" (*The Major Writings of Nichiren Daishonin*, vol. 5, p. 307).

A human lifetime is a succession of changes. What seemed changeless until yesterday may stand today at a fork in the road—beginning from this moment to change for the better or worse. What empower us amid this sea of change are guidelines that shed light on the correct path into the future and words of encouragement that revitalize us, especially in the midst of difficulty.

I, too, have words I have taken as mottoes to live by since my youth, such as:

> "A wave grows stronger with each obstacle it encounters"; and
> "Truly brave is the person who is strong when standing alone."

These are just two examples of the wisdom of our predecessors that I have applied to my struggles. For me, they have become sources of energy to overcome illness and poverty, engines to power my journey along the difficult path of religious and social reform that will guide people to happiness.

Even now that I am past seventy, the words with which my mentor, Josei Toda, encouraged me in my youth still resonate in my life.

Though engraved in my young heart so long ago, I can still hear them vividly in mind. Firmly grounded in Nichiren Daishonin's teachings, President Toda's profound view of life and his encouragement originating from his deep compassion served as a foundation for me to develop my character.

The spirit to encourage another is the spirit of a bodhisattva. In this sense, our Buddhist movement is an activity to resuscitate the heart of compassion that society has lost.

Lately, I have been giving addresses and writing poems to our friends in Japan and around the world almost every day. I do so with the prayer that happiness, victory and glory will forever be with those who wholeheartedly devote themselves to the Law and to the people.

This book came into existence as a result of strong requests from my friends in America. It contains excerpts from my addresses between 1990 and 1998. The SGI-USA editorial staff worked hard to select passages that stand on their own, that it is hoped can be of universal value to you, the reader, regardless of their original context.

Nothing will give me greater joy than if this book provides some meaningful direction for your precious life. Please allow me to express my heartfelt gratitude to those who helped in the translating, editing and compiling of the material in this book.

**DAISAKU IKEDA**

*May 3, 1999*

# EDITOR'S NOTE

WE ARE PLEASED TO OFFER THIS LATEST collection of daily encouragement drawn from SGI President Ikeda's addresses from 1990 through 1998. The editors selected the passages and, with few exceptions, randomly assigned them to dates. The reader therefore need not feel that a particular passage has special meaning for the date to which it was assigned. For dates significant to Nichiren Daishonin's life and the SGI, as well as for common U.S. holidays, the editors attempted to select passages that would be particularly appropriate for that day. Overall, we made a special effort to select passages that, even outside the specific context of the address, provide encouragement that can be considered universal.

We have also provided a detailed index and an appendix of the dates of the addresses from which the passages were selected. Throughout the text, references to *The Major Writings of Nichiren Daishonin* are abbreviated. The notation *MW-1, 161,* for instance, refers to *The Major Writings of Nichiren Daishonin*, vol. 1, p. 161.

Finally, we offer special thanks to Mr. Ikeda for allowing us to publish these excerpts, and we hope that *For Today and Tomorrow: Daily Encouragement* will become a treasured source of inspiration for years to come.

# JANUARY

# JANUARY 1

THOSE WHO WAKE UP EACH morning with work to accomplish and a mission to fulfill are the happiest people of all. SGI members are like this. For us each day is one of supreme purpose and satisfaction. For us each day is New Year's Day. Please exert yourselves vigorously with the determination to live each day to the fullest, so that you may compose a golden diary of life.

# JANUARY 2

THE PEOPLE ARE MOST IMPORTANT
and noble. President Toda was firmly
convinced of this point. And I have advanced
with the same spirit. This is also Nichiren
Daishonin's undying spirit. Please always
treasure and protect this organization of the
people that is the SGI.

1928:  Daisaku Ikeda, SGI president, is born.

# JANUARY 3

Eɪᴊɪ Yᴏsʜɪᴋᴀᴡᴀ (1892–1962), the renowned Japanese author of many epic historic novels, asserted, "Great character is forged through hardships." Surviving a life of hardships and difficulties, of stormy ups and downs, is what produces a person of great depth and character. True happiness is also found in such an unshakable state of life.

LIFE IS A SERIES OF CHANGES, a succession of ups and downs. But those who possess a prime point, a home to which they can return no matter what happens, are strong. To come home to the world of friendship in the SGI, to talk things over and prepare for a fresh departure—this is the way I hope all of you will live. When you do, you will advance upon a fundamentally unerring path to happiness.

# JANUARY 5

Faith is light. The hearts
of those with strong faith are filled with light.
A radiance envelops their lives. People with
unshakable conviction in faith enjoy a
happiness that is as luminous as the full moon
on a dark night, as dazzling as the sun on a
clear day.

# JANUARY 6

WE PRACTICE THIS BUDDHISM TO make our prayers and dreams come true and to achieve the greatest possible happiness. The purpose of Nichiren Daishonin's Buddhism is to enable us to realize victory. The fact that our prayers are answered proves the correctness of this teaching.

# JANUARY 7

WHEN WE PLANT THE SEED OF
happiness that is faith and carefully tend its
growth, it will produce fruit without fail.
We have to bear in mind, however, that we
cannot plant a seed today and expect it to
bear fruit tomorrow. That's not reasonable
and Buddhism is reason. If we persevere in
the practice of "faith equals daily life"
in accord with reason, then our prayers will
definitely be answered. This is Nichiren
Daishonin's promise to us. And his words
are true beyond any doubt.

# JANUARY 8

Prayer is the foundation. But at the same time if we fail to make concrete efforts, no matter how much daimoku we chant, our prayers will not be answered. Buddhism is reason. If we just chant without doing any work we cannot succeed in our jobs.

# JANUARY 9

THE REAL BENEFIT OF THE MYSTIC Law is inconspicuous. Just as trees grow taller and stronger year after year, adding growth rings that are imperceptible to the human eye, we too will grow toward a victorious existence. For this reason it is important that we lead tenacious and balanced lives based on faith.

# JANUARY 10

Buddhism is reason. It is vital, therefore, that our lives and our activities in society also accord with reason. Please manifest the principle of "faith equals daily life," so that you will be trusted, respected and emulated by others. Bringing fragrant flowers of trust and humanism to bloom throughout society is one of the goals of Buddhism. To do things that others find strange and unnatural, that run counter to common sense—such actions go against the basic tenets of Buddhism and amount to slander of the Law.

# JANUARY 11

THE ROLE OF LEADERS IS
important. Everything is determined by the
leaders' behavior. There is a passage in
*The Romance of the Three Kingdoms* that says
only those who possess genuine wisdom and
virtue win the highest regard from people. It
all comes down to you. You have to polish
and develop yourselves. Should there be a
leader or leaders in faith whom you do not
like, all you have to do is determine not to
become like them. All you have to do is
decide that you will become leaders who will
make everyone feel comfortable and at ease.

# JANUARY 12

In a passage of the "Record of the Orally Transmitted Teachings," the Daishonin observes, "When you bow to a mirror, the reflected image bows back" (*Gosho Zenshu*, p. 769). People who respect others are respected by others in turn. Those who are unstinting in their compassion and concern for others are also protected and supported by others. Our environment is essentially a reflection of ourselves.

# JANUARY 13

A LIFE LIVED WITHOUT PURPOSE
or value, the kind in which one doesn't know
the reason why one was born, is joyless and
lackluster. To just live, eat and die without any
real sense of purpose surely represents a life
pervaded by the world of Animality. On the
other hand, to do, create or contribute
something that benefits others, society and
ourselves and to dedicate ourselves as long as
we live up to that challenge—that is a life of
true satisfaction, a life of value. It is a
humanistic and lofty way to live.

# JANUARY 14

Everyone at some time suffers from illness in one form or another. The power of the Mystic Law enables us to bring forth strength to overcome the pain and suffering of sickness with courage and determination. The Daishonin writes: "Nam-myoho-renge-kyo is like the roar of a lion. What sickness can therefore be an obstacle?" (MW-1, 119).

# JANUARY 15

DOING GONGYO EVERY DAY IS A challenge. Introducing others to the practice is a challenge. Getting people to subscribe to our publications is a challenge. Attending meetings is a challenge. Sometimes it can all become too much and leave one feeling negative and wanting to take a break! Since we are human beings, it's only natural that we might feel this way on occasion. The important thing, however, is not to spin out of the orbit of faith. I hope you will continue to pursue the path of Buddhahood steadily and patiently, encouraging one another on your journey.

# JANUARY 16

It is important to take a long-range view. No great achievement is accomplished overnight or without difficulty. Should benefit be obtained easily without making any efforts in Buddhist practice, we'd probably just as easily abandon our faith and end up miserable as a consequence. Because it isn't easy to get into a highly ranked school, students study with all their might, gaining an abundance of knowledge and ability. Faith follows basically the same formula: Practice is essential to attaining Buddhahood.

PLEASE REMEMBER THAT PATIENCE is in and of itself a great challenge, and that it often holds the key to breaking through a seeming impasse.

# JANUARY 18

Dr. Martin Luther King Jr., who was a tireless crusader for human rights, said: "Life's most persistent and urgent question is, What are you doing for others?" Do not say you will do it "someday"; *now* is the time. Do not say "someone" will do it; *you* are the one. Now is the time for youth to take full responsibility and courageously pave the way for the people's triumph.

# JANUARY 19

SUFFERING AND UNDERGOING hardships for the sake of friends and for spreading the Law show the sense of responsibility of a genuine leader and are the behaviors of a bodhisattva. There is no suffering or hardship that a Bodhisattva of the Earth cannot surmount. So no matter what happens, I would like you to steadily advance one step at a time, always chanting Nam-myoho-renge-kyo with a vibrant voice.

In this lifetime, to
demonstrate the power of faith in the Mystic
Law to others, some of you may have been
born into poverty so that you could show
actual proof by gaining secure and
comfortable lives. Some of you may have been
born with ill health so that you could show
proof by growing strong and healthy.
Irrespective of your situations, however, the
light of faith in the depths of your beings will
continue to shine on eternally with
diamondlike brilliance.

# JANUARY 21

Humanity today lacks hope and vision for the future. It is for precisely this reason that the Bodhisattvas of the Earth have appeared. Without your presence, the future of humanity would be bleak and spiritual decline its destination. That is why you have been born in this age and are now playing an active role in society. This is the meaning of *jiyu*, or "emerging from the earth." Consequently, each of you will definitely become happy. Please be confident that you will lead lives overflowing with good fortune throughout the three existences of past, present and future.

# JANUARY 22

Ultimately, happiness rests on how you establish a solid sense of self or being. Happiness does not lie in outward appearances nor in vanity. It is a matter of what you feel inside; it is a deep resonance in your life. To be filled each day with a rewarding sense of exhilaration and purpose, a sense of tasks accomplished and deep fulfillment—people who feel this way are happy. Those who have this sense of satisfaction even if they are extremely busy are much happier than those who have time on their hands but feel empty inside.

# JANUARY 23

As PRACTITIONERS OF THE
Daishonin's Buddhism, we get up in the
morning and do gongyo. Some perhaps may
do so rather reluctantly! Nevertheless, doing
gongyo is itself a truly great and noble thing.
Gongyo is a solemn ceremony in which we
are looking out and over the universe.
It is a dialogue with the universe.

# JANUARY 24

WE USE OUR VOICES NOT ONLY TO chant daimoku but to guide, encourage and introduce others to the Daishonin's Buddhism. Our voice, therefore, is very important. An angry voice, a coarse voice, a cold voice, an imperious voice—none of these will communicate how wonderful Nichiren Daishonin's Buddhism is. I would like you to be humanistic leaders who can encourage others with bright warm voices, so that they will say, "What a lovely voice!" and "I'm always so inspired when I hear you speak." Becoming this kind of leader is one actual proof of your human revolution.

# JANUARY 25

THE IMPORTANT THING IS TO
hold on resolutely to one's convictions come
what may, just as the Daishonin teaches.
People who possess such unwavering
conviction will definitely become happy.

# JANUARY 26

Truly praiseworthy are those who resolve to work hard for kosen-rufu and the SGI within the lofty realm of Nichiren Daishonin's Buddhism. They are genuinely capable people. And they will definitely attain life-conditions of complete fulfillment.

SGI Day

1975:  Soka Gakkai International established; Daisaku Ikeda inaugurated as SGI president.

# JANUARY 27

Viewing events and situations
in a positive light is important. The strength,
wisdom and cheerfulness that accompany
such an attitude lead to happiness. To regard
everything in a positive light or with a spirit of
goodwill, however, does not mean being
foolishly gullible and allowing people to take
advantage of our good nature. It means
having the wisdom and perception to actually
move things in a positive direction by seeing
things in their best light, while all the time
keeping our eyes firmly focused on reality.

# JANUARY 28

ALL OF YOU ARE CHANTING FOR the happiness of many members—children of the Buddha—in your respective communities; you support and encourage them and work tirelessly on their behalf as if they were your own children. Your actions are truly those of great bodhisattvas; your state of life that of noble Buddhas.

# JANUARY 29

Pᴙᴀᴄᴛɪᴄɪɴɢ Bᴜᴅᴅʜɪsᴍ ᴍᴇᴀɴs being victorious. In advancing one step at a time amid the realities of our daily lives, in showing concrete actual proof, in becoming victors and successes, we are demonstrating with our very beings the validity of Nichiren Daishonin's Buddhism and serving as a source of hope and inspiration for those who will follow us on the path of faith.

# JANUARY 30

BUDDHISM TEACHES THAT "ALL phenomena in the universe are manifestations of the Law" (*Gosho Zenshu*, p. 564). I hope you will, with this understanding, engage in broad-ranging studies with vigor and determination. The brain has a potential as vast and boundless as the universe. How then do we manifest the brain's full creative powers? There is only one way to bring out our full intellectual capacity: by constantly putting our minds to work.

# JANUARY 31

Youth should not seek an easy comfortable path. No one develops in a pampered environment. Youth should instead actively seek out challenges and hardships, transforming them all into valuable assets as they strive to become individuals of outstanding character and ability.

# FEBRUARY

# FEBRUARY 1

Buddhism teaches that one characteristic of a bodhisattva is being able to perceive the world's sounds. The insight needed to correctly discern and grasp developments in society and the times— even to anticipate them before they happen— is indispensable.

# FEBRUARY 2

Because life is long, you should not be impatient. What matters most is that you embrace the Gohonzon throughout your life. It is vitally important to continually challenge yourself to chant even a little more daimoku and to pray before the Gohonzon for the fulfillment of your desires.

1987: SGI President Ikeda formally opens the World Peace Ikeda Auditorium, the first building designed and built specifically for SGI-USA activities.

# FEBRUARY 3

I CAN DECLARE WITH CONFIDENCE
that each of you who bravely exerts yourself
in doing Gakkai activities and taking
leadership for kosen-rufu, calmly overcoming
every obstacle along the way, will enjoy
immeasurable benefit. I can state with
certitude too that each of you is in perfect
accord with the Daishonin's spirit.
Your efforts win his unrestrained applause
and approval.

1987: Calabasas, Calif., campus of Soka University of
America, founded by SGI President Ikeda, opens.

# FEBRUARY 4

Please never turn your back on your faith. Courage is crucial. There is no room for faintheartedness in faith. The timid doom themselves to ridicule—from their partners, from their children, from their friends, from the world at large. The Daishonin declares that there is no place for cowards among his disciples. President Toda said the same.

# FEBRUARY 5

I HOPE THAT YOU WILL ALWAYS
speak the truth boldly, saying what needs to
be said no matter whom you're addressing.
When it comes to championing a just cause,
you must never be cowardly, never fawn,
never try to curry favor.

# FEBRUARY 6

UNLESS WE LIVE FULLY
right now, not sometime in the future, true
fulfillment in life will forever elude us. Rather
than putting things off till the future, we
should find meaning in life, thinking and
doing what is most important right now, right
where we are—setting our hearts aflame and
igniting our lives. Otherwise, we cannot
lead an inspired existence.

# FEBRUARY 7

YOUR ENVIRONMENT DOES NOT matter. Everything starts with you. You must forge yourself through your own efforts. I urge each of you to create something, start something and make a success of something. That is the essence of human existence, the challenge of youth. Herein lies a wonderful way of life always aiming for the future.

# FEBRUARY 8

I HOPE THAT AS LEADERS YOU WILL always express your appreciation for and do your utmost to support the many sincere members who are steadfastly exerting themselves in faith. The Daishonin says that when you see someone who embraces the Mystic Law, you should rise and greet them from afar, showing them the same respect you would a Buddha.

# FEBRUARY 9

THERE IS NO PLACE IN THE SGI for cowards or for egoists who are given to arbitrary or self-serving views. Our movement has no need for the fainthearted, filled with doubt, who readily succumb to negative influences. Let us strive for the Law and live with dignity as proud members of the SGI! The 21st century shall be the essential phase of our movement. Bathed in the brilliant light of dawn, let us take our places on that golden stage and lead truly magnificent lives!

# FEBRUARY 10

Kosen-rufu is a supreme, golden path extending throughout the Latter Day of the Law into the eternal future. Let us continue to advance boldly and intrepidly along this path as Nichiren Daishonin teaches. This is the way world peace will be accomplished. If we do not widely spread the principles and ideals of the Daishonin's Buddhism, there will be no hope for the peace and happiness of humankind.

# FEBRUARY 11

THE MOMENT WE RESOLVE "I WILL become healthy!" "I will become strong!" "I will work cheerfully for kosen-rufu!" our lives begin to move in that direction. We have to make up our minds.

1900: Josei Toda, the Soka Gakkai's second president, is born.

1996: Toda Institute for Global Peace and Policy Research founded by SGI President Ikeda in Tokyo; offices open in Hawaii in 1997.

# FEBRUARY 12

THE IMPORTANT THING IS TO HOLD firm to your beliefs without being influenced or swayed by what others do or say. Those who live this way are strong and free of regret. What matters most is how you lead your life— not what those around you are doing.

# FEBRUARY 13

Remembering things about
a person is an expression of compassion and
concern. Forgetfulness shows a lack
of compassion, a lack of responsibility.

# FEBRUARY 14

Strength is happiness.
Strength is itself victory. In weakness and
cowardice there is no happiness. When you
wage a struggle, you might win or you might
lose. But regardless of the short-term
outcome, the very fact of your continuing to
struggle is proof of your victory as a human
being. A strong spirit, strong faith and strong
prayer—developing these is victory and the
world of Buddhahood.

# FEBRUARY 15

LIFE IS FULL OF UNEXPECTED
suffering. Even so, as Eleanor Roosevelt said:
"If you can live through that [a difficult
situation] you can live through anything. You
gain strength, courage and confidence by
every experience in which you really stop to
look fear in the face. You are able to say to
yourself, 'I lived through this horror. I can
take the next thing that comes along.'" That's
exactly right. Struggling against great
difficulty enables us to develop ourselves
tremendously. We can call forth and manifest
those abilities lying dormant within us.
Difficulty can be a source of dynamic growth
and positive progress.

# FEBRUARY 16

I HOPE YOU WILL ALWAYS LIVE IN
unity with Nichiren Daishonin, pursuing faith
as disciples who are "of the same mind as
Nichiren." Unfazed by the petty jealousies of
others, please move forward boldly with joy
and laughter.

1222: Nichiren Daishonin is born.

# FEBRUARY 17

LIFE CONTAINS THE CAPACITY, like flames that reach toward heaven, to transform suffering and pain into the energy needed for value-creation, into light that illuminates darkness. Like the wind traversing vast spaces unhindered, life has the power to uproot and overturn all obstacles and difficulties. Like clear flowing water, it can wash away all stains and impurities. And finally, life, like the great earth that sustains vegetation, impartially protects all people with its compassionate, nurturing force.

# FEBRUARY 18

Religious strife must be avoided at all cost; under no circumstance should it be allowed. People may hold different religious beliefs, but the bottom line is that we are all human beings. We all seek happiness and desire peace. Religion should bring people together. It should unite the potential for good in people's hearts toward benefiting society and humanity and creating a better future.

# FEBRUARY 19

THIS LIFETIME WILL NEVER COME again; it is precious and irreplaceable. To live without regret, it is crucial for us to have a concrete purpose and continually set goals and challenges for ourselves. It is equally important that we keep moving toward specific targets steadily and tenaciously, one step at a time.

# FEBRUARY 20

In his later years, President
Toda often told his disciples: "Be courageous
in faith! No matter what other people may
say, advance boldly! Lead confident lives!
Make courage the Gakkai's eternal emblem!"
This was the spirit with which he charged us
before he died. Faith is the source of true
strength and courage. Without courage
and confidence we cannot be said to have
genuine faith.

# FEBRUARY 21

FRIENDSHIP IS STRONG.
Friendship, camaraderie and unity in faith lie
at the heart of the SGI. They come before the
organization. We must never make the
mistake of thinking that it is the other way
around. The organization serves as a means
for deepening friendship, comradeship
and faith. To confuse the means and the end
is a terrible mistake.

# FEBRUARY 22

WHAT WAS THE SECRET TO
Edison's success? He explained that it was to
never give up before he succeeded in what he
was trying to do. Not giving up—that's the
only way. Once you give up you are defeated.
This is equally true in the realm of faith.
Quitting is not faith. We have to keep
chanting until our prayers are answered.
That is the correct way of prayer.

# FEBRUARY 23

WITHOUT COURAGE WE CANNOT BE compassionate. Courage and compassion are inseparable, like the two sides of a coin. Faith is the wellspring of courage. The Daishonin says, "Nichiren's disciples cannot accomplish anything if they are cowardly" (MW-1, 128). A cowardly person cannot realize victory in life. Unless we have the courage to really dedicate our lives to kosen-rufu, we cannot construct true happiness for ourselves and others.

# FEBRUARY 24

Buddhism is not about leading a self-centered existence. If we do not base our lives on the Law, we are not practicing Buddhism. The German writer Friedrich von Schiller writes, "The brave man thinks upon himself the last." This is analogous to the spirit of not begrudging one's life taught in the Lotus Sutra. This means treasuring the Law more highly than one's life. The Law and kosen-rufu are central.

# FEBRUARY 25

GANDHI TAUGHT PEOPLE TO LIVE with lionlike courage, impressing upon them that they could not afford to leave things up to others, that they had to stand up for themselves and fight for justice. Ultimately, the only way forward is by developing self-reliance, forging a stand-alone spirit. That is the only path to victory.

# FEBRUARY 26

Buddhism TEACHES THAT LIFE AT each moment embraces all phenomena. This is the doctrine of a life-moment possessing three thousand realms, which is the Lotus Sutra's ultimate teaching and Buddhism's essence. Because of the profound way our lives interact with people around us, it is vital that we reach out to others, that we be engaged with our environment and with our local community. A self-absorbed practice or theory without action is definitely not Buddhism.

ORIGINALLY, EVERY PERSON'S LIFE
is a brilliantly shining mirror. Differences arise
depending on whether one polishes this
mirror: A polished mirror is the Buddha's life,
whereas a tarnished mirror is that of a
common mortal. Chanting Nam-myoho-
renge-kyo is what polishes our lives.

SGI-USA Women's Day

# FEBRUARY 28

You can forge the path to a
fulfilling and enjoyable life if you have the
depth of faith to regard everything as a source
for creating happiness and value. Conversely,
if you see everything only in a negative or
pessimistic light, your life will gradually but
inevitably be plunged into darkness.
Buddhism teaches the subtle principle of
*ichinen* and, moreover, the power of faith.

# FEBRUARY 29

WHEN PARENTS EXERT THEMSELVES
in the way of faith, they can lead their children
to happiness without fail. Likewise, the
attainment of Buddhahood of the child
guarantees the attainment of Buddhahood of
the parents. One lighthouse illuminates the
way for many ships to steer a course safely
through uncertain waters. In the same way,
people with strong and committed faith shine
as beacons of hope for their families.

# MARCH

# MARCH 1

WE NEED TO GO OUT AND MIX
with people every day. Making our local
community the base for our activities, we need
to forge ties of friendship with others and
work with them to create peace. Staying
connected in this way to our town, city, state
and country is a practical manifestation of our
lives permeating all things.

# MARCH 2

There is a saying, "To start an undertaking is easy; to maintain it is difficult." Though creating something new may seem daunting, it is in fact easy when compared to the far more challenging task of carrying on an existing enterprise, to keep it going, to develop it further. Everything depends on people, on capable successors. And our movement for kosen-rufu depends on young people. For that reason I am determined to do all that I can right now to raise genuine successors in the youth division.

# MARCH 3

WHAT IS YOUTH? THE FRENCH philosopher Roger Garaudy suggests that while most people believe a person is born young and then ages and dies, in reality, acquiring youth in the deepest sense is a very long and challenging process. The youth of which he speaks is the spiritual strength not to stagnate or grow resistant to change but to stay ever open to new possibilities. It is the power of the spirit that refuses to succumb to complacency and strives forward.

# MARCH 4

SHAKYAMUNI PROCLAIMS, "PEOPLE who are vigilant do not die; people who are negligent are as if dead." This is definitely true. Unremitting diligence in our Buddhist practice—brave and vigorous exertion—infuses our lives with the great life force of the eternal Buddha. In contrast, people who try to get by in life through cunning and deception enact a living death.

# MARCH 5

THE EFFORTS MADE BY ONE
individual can be immensely important.
Nichiren Daishonin repeatedly states that
victory depends not on numbers but on a
group or individual's attitude or resolve. In
one passage he writes: "Everyone in Japan,
from the sovereign on down to the common
people, all without exception tried to do me
harm, but I have survived until this day. This
is because, although I am alone, I have firm
faith [in the Lotus Sutra]" (MW-3, 198).
In other words, his strong faith enabled him
to emerge triumphant. I find this passage
deeply moving.

# MARCH 6

THERE IS NO NEED FOR YOU TO BE
impatient. If you can achieve something
very easily right from the start, you will find
no sense of fulfillment or joy. It is in making
tenacious, all-out efforts for construction
that profound happiness lies.

# MARCH 7

CALLING FORTH THE THREE powerful enemies and defeating them make one a votary of the Lotus Sutra. It is only natural, then, when we advance upon the correct path of mentor and disciple originating with the Daishonin, we will encounter obstacles. By battling the three powerful enemies, we become genuine disciples of the Daishonin. In that respect, the authenticity of the path of mentor and disciple followed by the first three presidents of the Soka Gakkai has been proven beyond doubt.

# MARCH 8

The great French philosopher Jean-Jacques Rousseau (1712–78) wrote in his work *Emile*: "There is no happiness without courage nor virtue without struggle." Without courage there is no happiness and it is impossible to create a life of value. This is an unchanging rule of human existence.

# MARCH 9

THE FUNDAMENTAL SPIRIT OF
Buddhism is that all people are equal. A
person is not great simply because of his or
her social standing, fame, academic
background or position in the organization.
In the world of faith, the truly great are those
who spread the Mystic Law and strive for
kosen-rufu, who actively work for the sake of
Buddhism and the happiness of others.
Supremely respectworthy are those who
champion the cause of kosen-rufu.

# MARCH 10

Where is happiness to be found? The famous Roman philosopher-emperor Marcus Aurelius (121–80) said, "A man's true delight is to do the things he was made for." Human happiness, he maintained, lies in doing those things only humans can: seeking the truth and acting to help those who are suffering. Goethe, too, asserted that those who work cheerfully and take joy in the fruits of their labor are truly happy. These are the words of great thinkers, and as you can see they are in complete accord with the teachings of Buddhism.

# MARCH 11

ALL RIGHT, LET'S GET TO WORK again!"—This is the spirit of people of genuine substance. Those who avoid hard work or neglect the things they have to do, who just while away their time, eating, sleeping, playing, watching television— such individuals will never experience true happiness, satisfaction or joy.

# MARCH 12

As SGI MEMBERS OUR WORK, OUR
mission, is clear. We have the unparalleled task
of working for the happiness of all humanity
in an endeavor we call kosen-rufu. To
participate in SGI activities and challenge
ourselves earnestly on the path of our mission
are the greatest happiness. It all comes down
to whether we can appreciate this point.

# MARCH 13

IF WE DON'T PRACTICE GONGYO, the rhythm of our lives will be thrown off kilter, just as a machine that isn't oiled will rust. Gongyo and chanting daimoku are like starting an automobile's engine every day and driving in the direction of happiness and truth. By doing so day after day, you will gradually attain perfect unity with the universe and the Law. That state is the state of the Buddha.

# MARCH 14

As SGI LEADERS, HOW WE
interpret the words of members and what we
say in response are important. A genuine
leader is someone who gives measured
thought to such matters. When talking with
individuals, ask yourselves: "What are they
worried about?" "What are they trying to
say?" "What are they thinking? "What is it
they seek?" Try to discern these things in
others. Try to know. Try to understand. This
is the challenge of leadership. From such
compassion arises wisdom.

# MARCH 15

WE MUST TAKE THE ENEMIES OF the Buddha to task. We absolutely cannot remain silent when we see people distorting and corrupting the Daishonin's teaching. To speak out resolutely and clarify what is correct and what is erroneous is the Soka Gakkai spirit. If we simply try to be amiable and avoid making waves, then we will play right into the hands of people with malicious intent.

# MARCH 16

MARCH 16, KOSEN-RUFU DAY.
The spirit of this day lies not in magnificent ceremonies or high-sounding words. It lies in being victorious. That is the most crucial thing in all endeavors. In life and in kosen-rufu, we either win or lose. I would like you to be absolute victors in both. No matter what excuses we try to make, giving in to defeat brings misery and loses us the respect of others. I hope each of you without exception will adorn your life with indestructible triumph.

Kosen-rufu Day

1958: More than 6,000 youth attend a ceremony at the head temple where President Josei Toda passes responsibility for the spread of the Daishonin's Buddhism to all youth division members.

# MARCH 17

You mustn't allow yourselves
to grow old before your time. Please live with
a youthful spirit. That is what Buddhism
teaches us to do, and it is how life ought to be
lived. If you make a commitment to work for
the sake of others, you will be rejuvenated.
If you devote your life to helping others,
you'll stay young. The power of
Nam-myoho-renge-kyo guarantees that.

# MARCH 18

LET US DO OUR UTMOST TO
sustain the wonderfully warm atmosphere of
the SGI—an atmosphere where members feel
free to discuss whatever is on their minds.
Unless we do so, our organization will stop
growing, stop developing. The SGI is a world
of humanity—of the heart, of faith, of
compassion. It is a world of unity and mutual
inspiration. That is why it is strong. If we
continue to value and promote these qualities,
the SGI will continue to grow and develop
forever. I want to declare here and now the
atmosphere where we can discuss anything is
fundamental to the SGI.

# MARCH 19

By DEVOTING OURSELVES
earnestly to SGI activities, we gain the ability
to turn all difficulties and obstacles into
benefit, recognizing that earthly desires and
delusions are enlightenment and that the
sufferings of birth and death are nirvana. No
matter how unpleasant the circumstances we
find ourselves in, we can transform them into
hope and good fortune—into eternal
happiness. How incredible this is!

THERE MAY BE TIMES WHEN LIFE
seems gloomy and dull. When we feel stuck in
some situation or other, when we are negative
toward everything, when we feel lost and
bewildered, not sure which way to turn—at
such times we must transform our passive
mind-set and determine, "I will proceed along
this path," "I will pursue my mission today."
When we do so a genuine springtime arrives
in our hearts, and flowers start to blossom.

# MARCH 21

Why is it that sometimes our prayers seem to not be answered? This is a manifestation of the Buddha's wisdom—so that we can deepen our prayers, become stronger people, live more profound lives and secure deeper, more lasting good fortune. If our slightest prayer were answered immediately, we'd become lazy and degenerate. And we couldn't hope to build a life of great dignity and substance.

# MARCH 22

I CALL TO EACH OF YOU:
Strive for prosperity! Strive for development!
Strive for victory! Life is about striving all out
to achieve our aims; it is about hard work and
effort. Regardless of how smart you may be,
intelligence alone cannot guarantee your
future.

# MARCH 23

Let us all set our sights on leading great lives dedicated always to truth and move toward that goal in good health, brimming with hope. Let us live our lives boldly, without regret, advancing with patience, enthusiasm and a genuine spirit of friendship and camaraderie.

# MARCH 24

WHEN WE PRACTICE GONGYO AND chant daimoku before the Gohonzon, the good and evil capacities of our lives begin to function as the exalted form of fundamental existence. Lives that are full of the pain of Hell, lives that are in the state of Hunger, lives warped by the state of Anger—such lives too begin to move in the direction of creating their own personal happiness and value. Lives being pulled toward misfortune and unhappiness are redirected and pulled in the opposite direction, toward good, when they make the Mystic Law their base.

# MARCH 25

WE ARE NO LONGER IN AN AGE
when one person can shoulder everything.
Of course, for the day-to-day running of the
organization someone will still be officially
designated as president, but ultimately our
future development hinges on every member
having the commitment required of a Soka
Gakkai president. With this spirit, this sense of
responsibility, this leadership in your activities,
may you always work for kosen-rufu and for
the victory of the people. May you also build
a Soka Gakkai where everyone can advance
joyfully, a Soka Gakkai of undying progress.

# MARCH 26

OF FOREMOST IMPORTANCE ARE
the people—not celebrities, the powerful, the
rich, scholars or others whom society deems
great or praiseworthy. The purpose of all
things must be the happiness of the people.
Everything else should be but a means to that
end. Those who fail to recognize this
fundamental point and look down on the
people and exploit them are thoroughly vile
and contemptible; they are a hindrance to
people's happiness.

# MARCH 27

WHILE CONTROLLING YOUR MIND, which is at once both extremely subtle and solemnly profound, you should strive to elevate your faith with freshness and vigor. When you do so, both your life and your surroundings will open wide before you and every action you take will become a source of benefit. Understanding the subtle workings of one's mind is the key to faith and attaining Buddhahood in this lifetime.

# MARCH 28

Youth must have the spirit to attack injustice, the spirit to refute that which is wrong, the spirit to spread the Daishonin's teaching. Just giving an appearance of promoting kosen-rufu and going with the flow, afraid of making waves, are the actions of self-serving youth, who are spiritually old and decrepit.

# MARCH 29

MOLLY BROWN WAS ON BOARD
the *Titanic* when it tragically sunk in 1912.
Although she knew the ship was taking on
water, she shouted to a panic-stricken fellow
passenger: "There's no danger. It simply can't
go down, because I'm on it and I'm
unsinkable." Her bantering words, which
rang out with the determination never to be
defeated and never to give in to despair are
said to have given courage to her fellow
passengers. Those who stand up at a crucial
moment demonstrate genuine greatness.

# MARCH 30

THERE ARE MANY ELEMENTS
involved in a prayer being answered, but the
important thing is to keep praying until it is.
By continuing to pray, you can reflect on
yourself with unflinching honesty and begin
to move your life in a positive direction on the
path of earnest, steady effort. Even if your
prayer doesn't produce concrete results
immediately, your continual prayer will at
some time manifest itself in a form greater
than you had ever hoped.

# MARCH 31

Position and appearances are
irrelevant. The important thing is to carry out
our personal duty, our commitment, no
matter what anyone else may say. This is a life
of true victory, a life of unsurpassed nobility
and fulfillment.

# APRIL

# APRIL 1

Emerson writes: "And so of cheerfulness, or a good temper, the more it is spent, the more of it remains." Cheerfulness is not the same as frivolousness. Cheerfulness is born of a fighting spirit. Frivolousness is the reverse side of cowardly escape. Emerson also said that "power dwells with cheerfulness; hope puts us in a working mood." Without cheerfulness there is no strength. Let us strive to advance still more brightly and cheerfully.

1974: SGI President Ikeda gives his first university lecture, at UCLA.

# APRIL 2

**W**HY ARE HUMAN BEINGS BORN?
This question has posed a great challenge.
President Toda lucidly set forward his
conclusion. Namely, that this world is a place
for people to, as the Lotus Sutra states, "enjoy
themselves at ease." We were born here in
order to thoroughly savor the joys of life.
Faith in the Daishonin's Buddhism is what
enables us to bring forth the great life force
we need to lead such an existence.

1958: Josei Toda, the Soka Gakkai's second president, dies.

# APRIL 3

FROM ONE PERSPECTIVE, GONGYO and daimoku are lyrics and songs. They are an ode to life. I hope, therefore, that your gongyo and daimoku will be such that even people who are not practicing will be favorably impressed by the sonorous and invigorating sound of your voices. That too will contribute to the spread of kosen-rufu.

# APRIL 4

THERE IS NO MEANS OTHER THAN
faith by which to open our lives and our inner
state of Buddhahood. Faith is the most
"open" state of mind of all. Infinite clusters of
good fortune spill forth from this unbarred
treasure house of life.

# APRIL 5

IN ALL THINGS PATIENCE IS THE
key to victory. Those who cannot endure
cannot hope to win. Ultimate triumph belongs
to those who can forbear.

# APRIL 6

THERE IS NO RETIREMENT AGE in faith. Sincere faith never ages. Those who exert themselves for the sake of the Law are ever young. Our heart is what matters most. Let us strive to the end of our days for kosen-rufu.

# APRIL 7

STRENGTH IS THE SOURCE OF happiness. We mustn't shy away from life's challenges. We mustn't be defeated. Refusing to be defeated equals victory. A person who perseveres to the end is a winner. In the course of promoting our movement, the Soka Gakkai has never pulled back in the face of any hindrance. We have kept moving forward. And that is the key to our success. Never to retreat a single step, no matter what—that is the Soka Gakkai spirit. Those who embrace this spirit can achieve unlimited victory.

# APRIL 8

GREAT INDIVIDUALS FIGHT ABUSES of authority. The truly strong do not lord it over the weak. People of genuine strength and courage battle against the powerful, the arrogant, the authoritarian, the evil and corrupt—all who look down on the people with contempt.

# APRIL 9

NOTHING IS WASTED IN FAITH.
One never loses out. Please be confident that
all your efforts to help others and promote
Buddhism are accumulating immense
treasures of good fortune in your life. This is
what is meant by inconspicuous benefit.

# APRIL 10

THE DAISHONIN'S WORDS ARE
guiding principles that have universal, eternal
relevance. It is important to study his
writings. And it is especially crucial that the
members of the youth division gain a solid
grounding in Buddhist study. The two ways
of practice and study are important. A
halfhearted attitude will not allow you to
complete these two paths. That would be a
truly sad thing.

# APRIL 11

As long as our mind of faith is connected to the Gohonzon, our benefits will never disappear. That's why it is vital for us to persevere in our Buddhist practice throughout our lives, no matter what, even if on some days our physical condition or other circumstances prevent us from doing gongyo and chanting daimoku to our full satisfaction. Those who continue to challenge themselves to the end savor ultimate victory.

# APRIL 12

Young people are the leaders of the twenty-first century. For that reason it is important that you have an understanding of history, that you can see through to the heart of things. A penetrating view of history is essential. A superficial one won't suffice.

# APRIL 13

QUITE SIMPLY, THERE CAN BE NO true democracy unless the citizens of a country realize that they are sovereign, that they are the main protagonists, and then with wisdom and a strong sense of responsibility take action based on that realization. Democracy cannot be successful in its mission unless the people rouse themselves to become more informed and involved, unless they unite, unless they establish an unshakable force for justice and keep a strict eye on the activities of the powerful.

# APRIL 14

Thoreau, a renowned American Renaissance thinker, wrote in his journal: "Nothing must be postponed. Take time by the forelock. Now or never! You must live in the present, launch yourself on every wave, find your eternity in each moment."
We shouldn't put anything off but seize the moment, living with all our being in the present. If we do that, he says, each moment will become eternity.

# APRIL 15

MATERIAL POSSESSIONS CANNOT be enjoyed after death. But millionaires rich in life force are able to freely make use of the treasures of the universe in lifetime after lifetime and enjoy a journey of eternal happiness. That is what constitutes proof of true victory in life.

# APRIL 16

SPENDING OUR TIME DOING WHAT
we please may bring momentary pleasure, but
it will not bring us true and lasting joy. We
cannot become great artists or great actors of
life—we cannot become great human beings.
Literature, music and drama are all to be
found in our activities for faith—in our
prayers, our challenges to develop ourselves
through SGI activities and our efforts to
educate others. All value is encompassed in
these activities. This is the profound realm of
Buddhism.

# APRIL 17

NOTHING CAN EQUAL THE
splendor of youth. To be young is to possess
a treasure of infinite worth, far greater than
any person of power. This is all the more true
of you who possess the eternal treasure of
the Mystic Law. Those who live based on this
supreme Law are bodhisattvas and Buddhas.

# APRIL 18

THOSE WHO ADVANCE TOGETHER
with this organization that is dedicated to
kosen-rufu and pervaded by benefit will
evolve the correct mind of faith that matches
the time. With this mind of faith you can fill
the canvas of your lives with portraits
of happiness in which all your wishes are
fulfilled.

# APRIL 19

AT A CRUCIAL MOMENT IT IS THE
strength and courage of ordinary people who
have no name or position in society that save
the day. The famous, the well-connected,
almost always have too much to lose, and they
abandon the cause in order to protect
themselves.

# APRIL 20

To possess both wisdom and compassion is the heart of our human revolution. If you have wisdom alone and lack compassion, it will be a cold, perverse wisdom. If you have compassion alone and lack wisdom, you cannot give happiness to others. You are even likely to lead them in the wrong direction, and you won't be able to achieve your own happiness.

# APRIL 21

Buddhism is reason.
It doesn't exist apart from society, apart from
reality. That is why it is important for each of
us to cultivate good judgment and common
sense. We must respect and harmonize with
society's ways. Respecting the life of each
individual, we work among the people. This is
the SGI's fundamental creed.

# APRIL 22

I HOPE YOU WILL ALWAYS HAVE
the spirit to learn with a lively curiosity and
interest. When leaders are enthusiastic to keep
on learning and growing, they inspire others.
New ideas emerge and spread. Fresh energy
to advance surges forth. Instead of pretending
to know all the answers, assuming an air of
wisdom, let us always strive for greater
understanding and insight into all manner of
things, so that we can continue learning
together and spur one another to grow. This
is the kind of spirit I want to cherish.

# APRIL 23

OUR FELLOW MEMBERS ARE ALL
family with whom we are linked by deep
bonds. If we support and protect this family,
they will act as protective forces in our
environment, supporting and keeping us from
harm in lifetime after lifetime. This is a
profound principle of Buddhism.

# APRIL 24

WHEN YOUTH ARE AWAKENED TO a sense of mission, their power is limitless. Ultimately, we have to entrust our hopes and visions for the future to the youth. This is a golden rule. Youth is pure. Youth will rise up to fulfill their ideals without calculation or self-interest. The fundamental spirit of a leader must be to reach out to such young people, work with them and bring out their capabilities and direct their youthful energies in a positive direction.

# APRIL 25

ADVERSITY GIVES BIRTH TO greatness. The greater the challenges and difficulties we face, the greater opportunity we have to grow and develop as people. A life without adversity, a life of ease and comfort, produces nothing and leaves us with nothing. This is one of the indisputable facts of life.

# APRIL 26

WHAT MATTERS IS WINNING IN the end; the wins and losses along the way are of secondary significance. It's final victory in life that counts and that is the reason for our Buddhist practice. No matter how powerful or famous or privileged a person might be, Nichiren Daishonin says, from a Buddhist point of view it is all nothing more than a dream, an illusory pleasure; true happiness can only be attained by revealing the state of Buddhahood within your own life.

# APRIL 27

AGE IS NOT AN EXCUSE FOR giving up. If you allow yourself to grow passive and draw back, it's a sign of personal defeat. There may be a retirement age at work, but there is no retirement age in life. How then could there be any "going into retirement" in the world of faith? The Buddhist Law is eternal, extending across the three existences of past, present and future, and one of the benefits of faith is perennial youth and eternal life.

# APRIL 28

HOW INCREDIBLE IT IS TO CHANT this wonderful daimoku each day! Nichiren Daishonin writes, "There is no greater happiness for human beings than chanting Nam-myoho-renge-kyo. The sutra [Lotus Sutra] says, 'The people there [in my land] are happy and at ease'" (MW-1, 161). There is no joy, happiness and ease surpassing what we can attain through chanting daimoku. No matter how much you may pursue the things you love and skip gongyo to have a good time—all such fleeting, worldly pleasures pale beside the deep sense of satisfaction that comes from chanting daimoku.

1253: Nichiren Daishonin chants Nam-myoho-renge-kyo for the first time.

# APRIL 29

WHAT IS SUCCESS IN LIFE?
Who are the truly successful? There are famous
and powerful people who become pitiful
figures in their old age. There are people who
die alone, feeling empty and desolate inside.
Just what is success? The English thinker
Walter Pater (1839–94) wrote: "To burn
always with this hard, gemlike flame,
to maintain this ecstasy, is success in life."
The person who lives life fully, glowing with
life's energy, is the person who lives a
successful life.

# APRIL 30

NOBEL LAUREATE GABRIELA
Mistral (1889–1957) of Chile was well
respected as a humanistic educator. Indicative
of the great spirit of compassion and caring
with which she interacted with her students is
her "Teacher's Prayer": "Let me be more
mother than the mother herself in my love
and defense of the child who is not flesh of
my flesh. Help me to make one of my
children my most perfect poem and leave
within him or her my most melodious melody
from that day when my own lips no longer
sing." With this same spirit, let us care for
and nurture young people.

MAY

# MAY 1

As you make your way home
tonight, may you pause for a moment to gaze
up at the night sky and let your heart
communicate with the moon in wordless
dialogue. Perhaps you might compose a poem
and set it down in your journal entry for
today. I would like you to possess such a
poetic spirit.

# MAY 2

No MATTER HOW HEALTHY,
intelligent or affluent we may be, if our minds
are weak, then our happiness will also be frail
and brittle. Our minds of faith, moreover,
enable us to bring out the full potential in all
things and situations, so it is crucial that we
strive to forge our minds of faith.

# MAY 3

As DIRECT DISCIPLES OF THE Daishonin, we have summoned forth the three powerful enemies of Buddhism. And defeating their schemes and repelling their onslaughts, we have carved out a great path of kosen-rufu. This has been the unrivaled pride of Mr. Makiguchi, Mr. Toda and myself as Soka Gakkai presidents. It is indisputable proof that the Soka Gakkai is the foremost organization in the entire world acting in accord with the Buddha's will and decree.

Soka Gakkai Day

1951: Josei Toda inaugurated as the second Soka Gakkai president.

1960: Daisaku Ikeda inaugurated as the third Soka Gakkai president.

# MAY 4

BUDDHISM CONCERNS ITSELF WITH winning. When we battle a powerful enemy, either we will triumph or we will be defeated—there is no middle ground. Battling against life's negative functions is an indivisible part of Buddhism. It is by being victorious in this struggle that we become Buddhas. We have to win. Moreover, Buddhism ensures that we can definitely do so.

# MAY 5

THIS IS WHAT I WOULD LIKE TO communicate to you, my young friends who are the heirs of the Soka legacy: Live out your lives together with the SGI, an organization fulfilling the Buddha's decree! Our activities in the organization of faith constitute our Buddhist practice, lead to the realization of kosen-rufu and enable us to carry out our human revolution. To think selfishly, "I'll just practice on my own and however I like" cannot be called correct faith. Such people are Buddhist in name only; they are not true practitioners.

# MAY 6

WE HAVE BOTH A WEAK SELF AND a strong self; the two are completely different. If we allow our weak side to dominate, we will be defeated. The thought, "I am still young and have a lot of time, so I can relax and take life easy" is a function of our weakness.

# MAY 7

MANY THINGS HAPPEN IN LIFE.
There are joyous days and times of suffering.
Sometimes unpleasant things occur. But that's
what makes life so interesting. The dramas we
encounter are part and parcel of being
human. If we experienced no change or
drama in our lives, if nothing unexpected ever
happened, we would merely be like
automatons, our lives unbearably monotonous
and dull. Therefore, please develop a
strong self so that you can enact the drama
of your life with confidence and poise in the
face of whatever vicissitudes you may
encounter.

# MAY 8

No one is more wonderful than a mother. And there is nothing more noble than a mother's heart. I hope you will all treasure your mothers. Truly praiseworthy are those who have a sense of gratitude and appreciation toward their parents. The Buddhist sutras teach that the practice of Buddhism is the ultimate expression of devotion to one's parents, and the Buddha excels in such dedication and concern.

# MAY 9

BUDDHISM IS CONCERNED WITH the essential nature of humanity. Buddhism is not found somewhere else separate from such beautiful expressions of humanity as appreciation toward one's mother and courtesy to others. As Nichiren Daishonin teaches in the Gosho, "behavior as a human being" that perfectly accords with reason is what constitutes the heart of Buddhism. Therefore, our world of faith must be a gathering that is full of affection and heartfelt consideration.

# MAY 10

THE STATE OF MIND WITH WHICH
we meet our death will greatly influence the
course of our lives over eternity. Granted, if
one is unconcerned by how one dies, or if one
dismisses any connection between this
existence and the next, then there probably
isn't any need to practice the Daishonin's
Buddhism. But the truth is that life is eternal,
that our existence continues even after we die.
Moreover, during the latent stage of death
before rebirth, we cannot change the essence
of our lives, we cannot carry out Buddhist
practice. Only while we are alive as human
beings can we practice Buddhism.

# MAY 11

THE DAISHONIN URGES US TO
earnestly chant Nam-myoho-renge-kyo, even
just once or twice, stressing that if we do so
we will definitely attain enlightenment. Now
some might immediately think: "All right! I'll
just put faith aside and take it easy, then
embrace faith seriously a year before I die."
But the Daishonin's words in this instance are
meant to spur his followers to devote greater
efforts to their Buddhist practice, emphasizing
the beneficial power of chanting even a
single daimoku. The correct way to read
the Gosho is to always interpret the
Daishonin's words from the standpoint
of strengthening our faith.

# MAY 12

I WANT YOU TO UNDERSTAND THE
subtle workings of the mind. How you orient
your mind, the kind of attitude you take,
greatly influences both you yourself and your
environment. The Buddhist principle of a
single life-moment encompassing three
thousand realms completely elucidates the
true aspect of life's inner workings. Through
the power of strong inner resolve, we can
transform ourselves, those around us and the
land in which we live.

# MAY 13

Dᴜʀɪɴɢ ᴏᴜʀ ᴅɪᴀʟᴏɢᴜᴇ,
Dr. Arnold Toynbee at one point told me that
his motto was *Laboremus*, Latin for "Let's get
to work!" Nichiren Daishonin's Buddhism
focuses on the present and future; it is infused
with the spirit, "Let's get started!" We
practice for the sake of the present and future.
It is important not to become trapped in the
past; we have to put it behind us. The
Buddhism of true cause is always based on the
present moment; it is always "from this
moment on."

# MAY 14

Kosen-rufu is a long-term struggle we are pursuing over the ten thousand years of the Latter Day. Therefore, as we strive to realize victory in the present, we need to maintain a vision of the next fifty or one hundred years. Each day I am making efforts with my focus on the infinite future.

# MAY 15

Ralph Waldo Emerson says,
"Good-nature is plentiful, but we want justice
with a heart of steel, to fight down the
proud." If people are merely good-natured,
then those who are arrogant and highhanded
will have free rein to carry on as they please.
Only those who fight with hearts of steel are
people of justice.

# MAY 16

Day in and day out. Today and again tomorrow. Moving of one's own accord to take action, to meet with people and conduct dialogues. This is what Shakyamuni did. Herein lies the correct way of life for human beings and the path of true honor for a Buddhist. This is the rhythm of the SGI's advance—an advance founded upon the same principles practiced and espoused by Shakyamuni and the original Buddha, Nichiren Daishonin.

Don't be dependent on anyone"—this is my sentiment. We each have to strengthen and develop ourselves through our own efforts. We must never surrender to any foe or difficulty. We must be fearless. This is the true spirit of self-reliance.

# MAY 18

THOSE WHO HAVE EXPERIENCED great suffering must win in life and become happy. If you're always losing and miserable, then you are not practicing the Daishonin's Buddhism correctly. You are not following the true path in life. Buddhism teaches the means by which the sad can become happy and the happy become happier still. That is the reason for our practice.

# MAY 19

From the standpoint of the eternity of our lives, because we embrace the Mystic Law everything is moving in a positive direction, everything contributes to our happiness and our attainment of Buddhahood. We need to have confidence in the Mystic Law; we mustn't be swayed by immediate circumstances or allow them to cloud our faith.

# MAY 20

WE MUSTN'T BE AFRAID OF
anything. It is important to remain firm in
our convictions. There is a great deal of
scheming and duplicity in the world. It is
foolish to allow ourselves to be swayed by
such things; it only leads to unhappiness. The
Mystic Law and Nichiren Daishonin are
absolutely free of any falsehood. Therefore,
to dedicate our lives to kosen-rufu is to lead
the wisest possible existence.

# MAY 21

WE MUST LIVE WITH VIBRANT hope. Nothing is stronger than hope. The Mystic Law is itself eternal hope. Happiness belongs to those who never despair, no matter what happens.

# MAY 22

WE NEED TO CULTIVATE A STATE
of life where we can thoroughly enjoy
ourselves at all times. We should have such joy
that even at the time of death we can declare
with a happy smile: "That was wonderful!
Where shall I go next?" This is the state of
mind of a person with strong faith. Such
individuals will be reborn without delay and
in a form and in a place exactly according with
their desires. Faith enables us to attain
the kind of generous and all-embracing state
of mind where we can enjoy everything
in our lives.

# MAY 23

WE NEED TO CULTIVATE THE
spirit to live with self-assurance, to make our
way joyously through life. We practice this
faith precisely to forge such a strong and
vibrant inner resolve.

# MAY 24

PRESIDENT TODA SAID: "THOSE who do not value the organization are practicing self-centered faith. With such faith you cannot expect to receive the truly profound benefits of this practice." Working hard within the organization for people's happiness and welfare is itself a truly noble Buddhist practice.

# MAY 25

THE HEART IS MOST IMPORTANT
of all. In his classic *The Little Prince*, the
French author Antoine de Saint-Exupéry
writes: "It is only with the heart that one can
see rightly; what is essential is invisible to the
eye." It is just as he says. We cannot always
tell whether something is genuine just with
our eyes. Only by looking with the heart can
we discern the true essence.

In Buddhism, we either win or lose—there is no middle ground. Now and in the future, let us advance, determined to win in every sphere of our lives. By winning in our lives, we are advancing kosen-rufu, and by advancing kosen-rufu, we win in our lives.

FORWARD! ALWAYS FORWARD!
This is a basic spirit of Buddhism. Nichiren
Daishonin's teaching is the Buddhism of true
cause. We live with our gaze fixed on the
future, not hung up on the past. To advance
eternally—this is the essence of life and the
essence of what it means to be a practitioner
of the Daishonin's Buddhism.

# MAY 28

WHAT IS TRUE JOY IN LIFE?
This is a difficult question—and one that
has occupied a great many thinkers and
philosophers. Joy can quickly give way to
suffering. Joy is short and suffering long. Also
what passes for joy in society is superficial. It
cannot compare with the joy deriving from
the Mystic Law. The key then lies in
cultivating a state of mind where we can
declare without reservation that life itself is
a joy. This is the purpose of our Buddhist
practice.

# MAY 29

We who embrace the Mystic Law will not suffer on account of old age or death. As long as we keep the flame of faith alive, the fire of life force will forever burn brightly within us; we can live with great confidence transcending birth and death. Faith is the engine that enables us to live with hope throughout our lives.

# MAY 30

THOSE WHO MAKE MANY FRIENDS have greater opportunities for growth and self-development; as such they make society a better place and lead happy, satisfying lives. In every situation, human relations— communication and personal interaction—are vital. We need to initiate and nurture friendships and contacts with many people, both within the organization and in society at large. Our lives will open and be enriched to the extent that we do so.

# MAY 31

Buddhism is about bringing happiness, joy and fulfillment to all. It enables us not only to become happy ourselves but to make causes for the enlightenment of our ancestors seven-plus generations back and for the happiness and prosperity of our children, grandchildren and descendants throughout future generations. This is the great benefit of Buddhism.

# JUNE 1

A COWARD CANNOT BECOME A
Buddha. We cannot attain Buddhahood
unless we possess the heart of a lion.
The harsher the situation, the bolder the
stand we must take. This is the essence of the
Soka Gakkai spirit.

No MATTER WHERE WE GO, WE
cannot escape from the sufferings that are
part and parcel of life. If we cannot avoid
these sufferings, then our only choice is to
overcome them. And since we have no choice
but to overcome them, then we might as well
live joyfully and vigorously while doing so.
Let's continue to strive and chant daimoku
to the end.

# JUNE 3

I WOULD LIKE EACH OF YOU TO rise to the challenge of revolutionizing the area where you live into an ideal community and to do so with the determination to start from where you are right now. This means building a good SGI organization in your local area—and building it yourself with loving, painstaking care, the way an artist pours his or her heart and soul into creating a work of art. It also means fostering capable people. Buddhism, after all, can only flourish if there are people who uphold and practice its teachings.

# JUNE 4

DEATH WILL COME TO EACH OF US some day. We can die having fought hard for our beliefs and convictions, or we can die having failed to do so. Since the reality of death is the same in either case, isn't it far better that we set out on our journey toward the next existence in high spirits and with a bright smile on our faces—knowing that in everything we did, we did the very best we could, thrilling with the sense "That was truly an interesting life"?

# JUNE 5

COWARDICE IS HARMFUL FOR IT
delights the enemies of Buddhism and
obstructs the advance of kosen-rufu. The
fainthearted cannot savor the true benefit of
faith; their ability to tap the power of the
Buddha and the power of the Law [of the
Gohonzon] in their lives is enfeebled.

# JUNE 6

SCIENCE IS BASED ON TESTED proof or empirical evidence. You conduct a test or experiment and then observe the results. Nichiren Daishonin's Buddhism, similarly, teaches that nothing beats actual proof. In this regard, it stands alone among the religions of the world. I hope that each year you will strive to show clear proof of victory in Buddhism and your studies. Please always remember that showing such proof is the mark of a true successor.

1871: Tsunesaburo Makiguchi, the Soka Gakkai's first president, is born.

# JUNE 7

FAITH AND DAILY LIFE, FAITH AND work—these are not separate things. They are one and the same. To think of them as separate—that faith is faith, and work is work—is theoretical faith. Based on the recognition that work and faith are one and the same, we should put one hundred percent of our energy into our jobs and one hundred percent into our faith, too. When we resolve to do this, we enter the path of victory in life. Faith means to show irrefutable proof of victory amid the realities of society and in our own daily lives.

# JUNE 8

PRESIDENT TODA OFTEN SAID THAT the final four or five years of one's life are decisive. No matter how good the preceding years may have been, one's life ends in defeat and sadness if the final few years are miserable. On the other hand, someone whose last four or five years are happy and filled with joy can be described a winner in life. No matter what happens, even if we should fall sick, we must never grow discouraged or allow ourselves to be defeated. This is vital. As long as our spirits are undefeated, we are victors.

WE HAVE TO MAKE OURSELVES
heard. We have to speak out for what we
believe in. When we, the people, boldly state
our true convictions—never losing our
optimism or sense of humor—the times will
change. When it comes to speaking out for
justice, there isn't any need for restraint. On
the contrary, to be reserved or hesitant under
such circumstances is wrong.

# JUNE 10

WHEN SOMETHING NEEDS SAYING, it is our duty to speak out. When something is right, we should say so; and when something is wrong or mistaken, we should likewise point it out. Cheating, lies or scheming should be denounced with alacrity. It is precisely because we have done this that the Soka Gakkai and the SGI have developed to the extent they have. To say what must be said— that is the spirit of propagation and the essence of the Soka Gakkai and the SGI.

# JUNE 11

THIS IS THE ERA OF YOUTH.
Youth do not depend on anyone. Nor do they
hang on someone else's coattails. "I will
open the way forward myself. I will advance
kosen-rufu. I will see to it that the SGI is
victorious." This is the spirit of youth and the
attitude of true successors who love and
cherish the SGI.

# JUNE 12

Education definitely changes people's lives. This is why the SGI is so earnest when it comes to Buddhist study, which is the highest field of learning; it is the study of human beings and the foremost education. Buddhist study is the soul of the SGI.

# JUNE 13

It all comes down to hope.
If we SGI members advance with hope and
buoyant spirits, then we have nothing to fear
in either the present or the future. The Law
will continue to spread as long as those who
uphold it remain vigorous and well.

# JUNE 14

CHANTING DAIMOKU IS THE
foundation of the Daishonin's Buddhism.
When we chant sonorous daimoku, the sun
rises in our hearts. We are filled with power.
Compassion wells forth. Our lives are lit with
joy. Our wisdom shines. All Buddhas and
Buddhist deities throughout the universe go
to work on our behalf. Life becomes
exhilarating.

# JUNE 15

THE DAISHONIN TEACHES THE
meaning of true happiness and the true
purpose of life. Fame and momentary glories
are no more than illusions. True happiness lies
in cultivating the great state of Buddhahood
within one's life. This is life's true purpose. By
chanting daimoku, we can change all of our
sufferings into the ingredients for attaining a
Buddha's lofty state of life.

# JUNE 16

ONE OF MY FAVORITE ARGENTINE
poets, the great educator Almafuerte
(1854–1917), wrote: "To the weak, difficulty
is a closed door. To the strong, however, it is
a door waiting to be opened." Difficulties
impede the progress of those who are weak.
For the strong, however, they are
opportunities to open wide the doors to a
bright future. Everything is determined by
our attitude, by our resolve. Our heart is what
matters most.

# JUNE 17

Hოw exhilarating it is to stand tall, walk with a buoyant step and be flexible in one's actions! How attractive to those we meet are our sparkling eyes and vibrant voices! This is the principle of the true entity of all phenomena. Your fresh and vital appearance eloquently attests to the greatness of faith, and you will find that you naturally cultivate a sphere of friendship and understanding among those around you.

# JUNE 18

THE GREAT AMERICAN POET
Walt Whitman writes in *Leaves of Grass*: "All
comes by the body, only health puts you
rapport with the universe." I am sure you are
all very busy, but I hope you will advance in
good health and with optimism and enjoy the
power of your faith, which is what puts you in
rhythm with the universe.

# JUNE 19

I HOPE THAT YOU WILL LEAD immortal, invincible and joyous lives, filled with confidence, pride and good cheer. I also hope you will display inspiring leadership, while doing your utmost to protect your respective areas.

1996: The Florida Nature and Culture Center opens.

# JUNE 20

YOUR FAITH GUARANTEES THAT AN infinite number of your ancestors and descendants will attain Buddhahood. Such is the wondrous power of the Mystic Law. How profound and important is your existence! There is also no greater way to repay the debt of gratitude to your parents than through faith.

# JUNE 21

WHEN YOU DEVOTE YOUR LIFE TO
achieving your goal, you will not be bothered
by shallow criticism. In fact nothing
important can be accomplished if you allow
yourself to be swayed by some trifling matter,
always looking over your shoulder and
wondering what others are saying or thinking.
The key to achievement is to move forward
resolutely along your chosen path.

# JUNE 22

It's foolish to be obsessed with past failures. And it's just as foolish to be self-satisfied with one's small achievements. Buddhism teaches that the present and the future are what are important, not the past. It teaches us a spirit of unceasing challenge to win over the present and advance ever toward the future. Those who neglect this spirit of continual striving steer their lives in a ruinous direction.

# JUNE 23

JESSE OWENS, WHO WON FOUR
gold medals at the 1936 Berlin Olympics,
later remarked that one's inner life is the true
Olympics. Life itself is an Olympics where we
strive each day to better our own personal
records.

# JUNE 24

You must be strong. There is no hope of winning in this chaotic world if you are weak. No matter what others do or say, it is important to develop your ability and then put that ability to use. Strong faith, of course, is the best means for drawing out one's inner strength. You each have a very important mission, and I hope you will awaken to and be proud of that mission.

# JUNE 25

We LIVE IN AN AGE WHERE
opportunities for profound life-to-life
inspiration are all but nonexistent.
Idle amusements bring only fleeting pleasure.
They produce neither profound inspiration
nor growth for one's life. By contrast,
Buddhism exists to enable people to realize
personal growth and to improve their lives.
Buddhism is always rooted in the reality of
life. It is the wellspring of wisdom for
bringing harmony and happiness to our
families, local communities and
society at large.

# JUNE 26

THIS SPIRIT OF ENGAGING OTHERS in dialogue on equal terms is the essence of Buddhism. Ordering people about in a high-handed, arrogant manner, shouting at them to do one's bidding, is truly deplorable behavior. Such a world has no relation to Buddhism. Through dialogue Shakyamuni opened hearts that were closed, softened hearts that had grown hard and melted hearts that were frozen.

# JUNE 27

In a world where indifference and inhumanity prevail, let us use our discussion meetings as the pivot for creating oases of peace and harmony in our homes and in our local communities and then extending them to encompass every sphere of society.

# JUNE 28

In the "Record of the Orally
Transmitted Teachings," the Daishonin says,
"One should regard meeting obstacles as true
peace and comfort" (*Gosho Zenshu*, p. 750).
You may wonder how encountering obstacles
could be a source of peace and comfort. But
the truth of the matter is that through
struggling against and overcoming difficulties,
we can transform our destiny and attain
Buddhahood. Confronting adversity,
therefore, represents peace and comfort.

# JUNE 29

THE IMPORTANT THING IS TO
advance brightly and strive to be victorious at
each moment, right where we are; to begin
something here and now instead of fretting
and worrying over what will happen. This is
the starting point for transforming our lives.

# JUNE 30

THE PLACE WHERE WE ARE RIGHT
now is what matters. This is all the more true
for us who embrace the Mystic Law.
Buddhism teaches that we can transform
wherever we are into the Land of Eternally
Tranquil Light.

JULY

# JULY 1

NAM-MYOHO-RENGE-KYO IS LIKE the roar of a lion," the Daishonin says (MW-1, 119). It is by chanting powerful daimoku, like a lion's roar, that we can move the Buddhist deities, the protective forces of the universe. The voice is very important—it has profound power. While naturally being careful not to disturb your neighbors, I hope you will endeavor to chant cheerful and powerful daimoku that reaches all the Buddhist deities and Buddhas throughout the ten directions.

# JULY 2

THE WRITER GOETHE WAS AN unflagging optimist. How was he able to maintain such optimism? Because he was always active. He did not allow his life to stagnate. He writes: "It is better to do the smallest thing in the world than to hold half an hour to be too small a thing." Spending thirty minutes a day assiduously challenging some undertaking can completely change our lives.

# JULY 3

THOSE WHO HAVE A MENTOR IN
life are truly fortunate. The path of mentor
and disciple is one that leads to personal
development and growth. Those without a
mentor may appear free and unbeholden to
anyone, but without a solid standard or model
on which to base themselves their lives will
be aimless and wandering.

Day of Mentor and Disciple

1945: President Josei Toda is released from Toyotama
Prison.

1957: Daisaku Ikeda is arrested in Osaka on false charges.

# JULY 4

I PLACE A HIGH VALUE ON
personal initiative. Kosen-rufu will be
advanced by brave people armed with the
spirit of independence who voluntarily strive
to fulfill the vow they made in the remotest
past. Because they struggle of their own
volition, they have no complaints or
grievances. The greater the obstacles they
face, the greater the courage, wisdom and
power they muster from within.

# JULY 5

WHAT DOES ATTAINING
Buddhahood mean for us? It does not mean
that one day we suddenly *turn into* a Buddha
or become magically enlightened. In a sense,
attaining Buddhahood means that we have
securely entered the path, or orbit, of
Buddhahood inherent in the cosmos. Rather
than a final static destination at which we
arrive and remain, achieving enlightenment
means firmly establishing the faith needed to
keep advancing along the path of absolute
happiness limitlessly, without end.

# JULY 6

WE COULD LIKEN DOING GONGYO and chanting daimoku to the Earth's rotation on its axis, while taking part in activities resembles the Earth's revolution around the Sun. To enter this path, which enables us to savor a state where life is an unparalleled joy, is itself proof of our attainment of Buddhahood. In the present age, SGI activities represent the means by which we can attain Buddhahood.

# JULY 7

Vital are wisdom, tenacity and self-expression, as well as the strong life force that makes these things possible. Buddhism is an earnest struggle to win. This is what the Daishonin teaches. A Buddhist, therefore, must not be defeated. I hope you will maintain an alert and winning spirit in your work and daily life, taking courageous action and showing triumphant actual proof time and again.

# JULY 8

WE MUST MAKE STEADY AND
persistent efforts firmly grounded in daily life.
If we travel in the orbit of "faith equals daily
life," all our prayers will definitely be
answered. We can then lead lives in which all
our desires will be fulfilled. Should all our
prayers be answered without our having to
make any effort, we would grow lazy. Should
all our desires be achieved without our ever
having to experience suffering or hardship, we
could not understand the pain and struggles
of others, and our compassion would
gradually wane.

# JULY 9

Even in times of hardship, the important thing is for each of us to determine that we are the star, protagonist and hero of our lives and keep moving forward. Putting ourselves down and shrinking back from the obstacles looming before us spell certain defeat. Through making ourselves strong and developing our state of life, we can definitely find a way through. As long as we uphold the Mystic Law throughout our lives, we can break through any impasse and surmount any obstacle. We will also be able to lead all those who are suffering to happiness.

# JULY 10

Beethoven is called a genius. But we need to be aware that his genius was based on incredibly strenuous effort. It all comes down to hard work, to tenacious efforts. You cannot become a person of the highest caliber if you have a casual, easygoing attitude, thinking things will somehow just fall into place. Accordingly, Beethoven's motto was "No day without a line." Every day without fail, he wrote music. He would not let even a single day pass without working assiduously. To continue every day—this is just like our practice of gongyo. Making persistent efforts each day is a source of tremendous strength.

# JULY 11

It is important that youth in particular actively seek challenges to forge and strengthen themselves. Those who enjoy material luxury from a young age and do not work hard cannot become people of outstanding character. They cannot become great leaders who protect the people. I hope that you will work hard, sparing no effort, and develop yourselves as indomitable champions, shaken or disheartened by nothing.

1951: Young men's division established.

# JULY 12

I IMAGINE THAT SOME OF YOU have family members who are not yet practicing Nichiren Daishonin's Buddhism. There is no need to be impatient or to agonize over this. Whether people take faith has to do with their mystic connection with Buddhism, which takes a variety of forms. Important is the presence of one person who is practicing. One person's attainment of Buddhahood brings happiness to family members and all those around him or her. When a single sun rises, everything is illuminated.

# JULY 13

THE GLORY WE ENJOY IN A DREAM vanishes without a trace when we awaken. When an illusion disappears, nothing is left of its joy except a sense of emptiness, like that which one feels when finally sobering from a state of drunkenness. The joy of Buddhahood, however, is profound, indestructible and everlasting.

# JULY 14

GOVERNMENTS COME AND GO, economies rise and fall and society constantly changes. Only the good fortune that we accumulate during our lives lasts forever. The true victors are those who cultivate the tree of Buddhahood in the vast earth of their lives, while achieving success both in society and their personal lives through true faith and a true way of living.

# JULY 15

WHAT IS THE TREASURE OF YOUTH?
It is struggle; it is hard work. Unless you
struggle, you cannot become truly strong.
Those who fight hard during their youth will
have nothing to fear when the time comes to
put the finishing touches on their lives. They
will possess a great state of life that towers
strong and unshakable. In Buddhism, we call
this the state of Buddhahood, which nothing
can undermine or destroy. It is a state of mind
enjoyed by invincible champions of life.

# JULY 16

THE POWERFUL MAY APPEAR GREAT, but in reality they are not. Greatest of all are the ordinary people. If those in power lead lives of idle luxury it is because the people are silent. We have to speak out. With impassioned words, we need to resolutely attack abuses of power that cause people suffering. This is fighting on the side of justice. It is wrong to remain silent when confronted with injustice. Doing so is tantamount to supporting and condoning evil.

1260: Nichiren Daishonin submits his treatise "On Establishing the Correct Teaching for the Peace of the Land."

# JULY 17

Life isn't always smooth. If it were, we would never grow and develop as human beings. If we succeed, we are envied; if we fail, we are ridiculed and attacked. Sadly, this is how people are. Unexpected grief and suffering may lie ahead of you. But it is precisely when you encounter such trying times that you must not be defeated. Never give up. Never retreat.

# JULY 18

THERE IS NO NEED TO SEEK
impatiently for greatness, fame or wealth. The
Earth and Sun do not hurry; they follow their
own path at their own pace. If the Earth were
to accelerate and complete one rotation in
three hours instead of twenty-four, we would
be in big trouble! The most important thing
in life, too, is to find a sure and certain path
and confidently advance along it.

# JULY 19

$Y$OUTH IS A TRULY WONDERFUL thing. Unfortunately, though, this is often something that's hard to appreciate when we're young. Life passes by quickly. Before we know it, we are old. That's why in our youth we should be as active as we possibly can. Rather than a life of blank pages, live a life crammed full of memories—of battles well fought and wonderfully diverse experiences. Not to leave behind any history, to just grow old and die, is a sad way to live.

1951: Young women's division established.

# JULY 20

OUR LIVES ARE RULED BY impermanence. But simply realizing that changes nothing. There is no value in bleak pessimism. The challenge is how to create something of enduring value within the context of our impermanent lives. The Lotus Sutra teaches us how to do this.

# JULY 21

TRUE AND LASTING HAPPINESS
only and always comes from our own efforts,
our own wisdom, our own good fortune. This
is a fundamental truth. Faith is the key to
strengthening our efforts, wisdom and good
fortune; SGI activities are the key to
strengthening ourselves.

# JULY 22

Without practice or actual efforts, there is no bodhisattva. Action is the essence of a Buddha. A self-centered life lived solely in pursuit of one's own benefit and fortune is empty and base. A Bodhisattva of the Earth, in contrast, respects others and works for their happiness.

# JULY 23

IF WE ATTAIN THE STATE OF Buddhahood in this lifetime, that state will forever pervade our lives. Throughout the cycle of birth and death, in each new lifetime, we are endowed with good health, wealth and intelligence, along with a supportive, comfortable environment, and lead lives that overflow with good fortune. Each of us will also possess a unique mission and be born in an appropriate form to fulfill it.

# JULY 24

Our lives are our own. It is not for someone else to dictate to us how we should live them. All that awaits those who allow themselves to be continually swayed by what other people say or do is unhappiness. We simply need to have the self-belief to be able to say: "This is right. This is the path I will follow. I am content." Happiness is born from such inner fortitude. Moreover, those who earnestly devote themselves in accord with the Mystic Law cannot fail to realize lives of total fulfillment.

# JULY 25

BUDDHISM IS, IN A SENSE, AN
eternal struggle between the Buddha and
demons; in other words, a contest between
positive and negative forces. If we are never
assailed by negative influences, we cannot be
said to be truly practicing Nichiren
Daishonin's Buddhism. Buddhist practice lies
in bravely facing and overcoming adversity.

# JULY 26

FAITH IS PERSEVERANCE. THE KEY
to victory in any struggle in life is persistence.
That is why Nichiren Daishonin stresses the
importance of having faith that flows
ceaselessly like water rather than faith that
flares up briefly like fire. To advance
continuously, it is important never to become
exhausted. Carrying out activities until late at
night does not equate with strong faith.

# JULY 27

BUDDHISM IS FOUND IN THE reality of society and daily life. Because Buddhism is in no way separate from this reality, we must strive through our actions to be exemplary models for others.

LIFE IS A PROCESS OF ONGOING
challenge. Those who lead lives of boundless
challenge realize boundless growth. In a time
of tumultuous change, what people need
most are the vitality to challenge their
circumstances, the wisdom to open the
treasure house of knowledge, and
to strive ceaselessly to create value.

# JULY 29

THE ULTIMATE ESSENCE OF
Nichiren Daishonin's Buddhism lies in living
on through to the very end, pressing ever
forward, courageously taking on each new
challenge we encounter and never giving up.
Constructing eternal glory—the state of
Buddhahood—within our own lives is the
purpose of our Buddhist practice in this
lifetime; hence the Daishonin's constant
urging that we make tenacious efforts in the
present.

# JULY 30

Faith enables us to secure ultimate victory. It enables us to live with vigor and joy and to strive to improve ourselves—to become the very best people we can be. Moreover, faith enables us to walk through life with complete assurance and confidence, unafraid of anything.

# JULY 31

WHAT IS THE SECRET TO VICTORY?
Mr. Toda once described that in a certain
sense life is a gamble. "If you are lucky, you
will win," he said. "But if you are unlucky,
then sometimes no matter how hard you try
you lose. This is a hard fact." That is why, in
addition to ability, good fortune is essential.
The key to creating good fortune is found in
faith and daimoku. I hope that you will all act
in accord with the fundamental Law of
Buddhism and lead victorious lives filled with
unsurpassed good fortune.

# AUGUST

# AUGUST 1

WE MUST NOT ALLOW OURSELVES
to become bureaucratic and take for granted
the efforts of those working behind the
scenes. Nor must we ever forget to be
considerate of those members of our families
who may not be practicing the Daishonin's
Buddhism. We must remember that for every
person involved in SGI activities there is
another, supporting him or her behind the
scenes.

# AUGUST 2

THE GREATER OUR EFFORTS TO advance kosen-rufu, the greater the benefit and eternal good fortune we will accumulate in our lives. The more outstanding people we can foster, the stronger and healthier we will become. The more aware we are of our responsibility, the more joy we will experience. Such are the workings of the Buddhist Law.

# AUGUST 3

As HUMAN BEINGS, LET US REACH beyond our small, limited selves and attain an all-encompassing state of being, our hearts communing with the vast universe.

# AUGUST 4

THE RESOLVE TO ACCOMPLISH
your goals is what counts. If you earnestly put
your mind to something, your brain, your
body, your environment—everything—will
start working toward achieving that end.

# AUGUST 5

WE CANNOT BUILD TRUE
character if we allow ourselves to be swayed
by passing praise or censure. "Don't concern
yourself with petty criticisms! Commune
constantly with fine books and fine people
and improve yourself!" This was the creed by
which Mr. Makiguchi and Mr. Toda lived
their lives.

# AUGUST 6

Youth, and indeed life itself, flash by in the blink of an eye. That is why it is important for you to ask yourselves what you can do for those who are suffering, what you can do to resolve the mournful contradictions that plague society, and boldly take on these great challenges without shunning the problems and difficulties you will inevitably face.

# AUGUST 7

Gandhi stressed the importance of being resolute in one's determinations: "A man who says that he will do something 'as far as possible' betrays either his pride or his weakness, though he himself may attribute it to his humility. There is, in fact, not a trace of humility in such an attitude of mind." In short, he asserts that someone who makes halfhearted pronouncements is either arrogant or cowardly.

# AUGUST 8

The present, as I am sure you all sense, is an age pervaded by great weariness and apathy. I would like you to be aware that the power and energy to serve humanity in such an enervated age can only be born from a vigorous, indomitable, noble will. Though the times may be rife with petty human conflicts, a pervading sense of hopelessness and all manner of turbulent storms, I hope that all of you will forge ahead boldly with unflagging good cheer.

# AUGUST 9

THE COURSE OF OUR LIVES IS
determined by how we react—what we decide
and what we do—at the darkest of times. The
nature of that response determines a person's
true worth and greatness.

# AUGUST 10

From one perspective, Buddhist practice means plunging into the midst of the people and striving to strengthen our life force to the greatest extent. The purpose of SGI activities is for each of us to be able to build a strong, invincible, diamondlike self that can overcome every difficulty and blaze a way forward wherever we go. Obstacles are a golden opportunity to quickly forge an inner self that is as indestructible as a diamond, able to endure for eternity.

# AUGUST 11

Let's read the Gosho regularly. Even just a little is fine. Even a single sentence. Just opening the Gosho is a start. At any rate, let's strive to read the Daishonin's writings. It's important to have the spirit to study the Gosho, to open up the Gosho. Even if you forget what you've read, something profound will have been engraved in the depths of your life.

# AUGUST 12

COURAGE IS FREE. ANYONE CAN have it. Courage is another name for the SGI spirit. Mr. Toda said: "The Buddha is filled with compassion, but it is hard for us common mortals to show compassion. So we must have courage instead." In other words, when we work courageously for kosen-rufu, our actions by their very nature become compassionate.

# AUGUST 13

AN IMPORTANT THING IS THAT you concentrate on developing yourself. Whatever others may say or do, those who have established their own solid identity will triumph in the end. The great Japanese author Eiji Yoshikawa (1892–1962) wrote in his novel *Miyamoto Musashi* [an account of the seventeenth-century master swordsman of the same name]: "Rather than worrying about your future, thinking 'Perhaps I should become this or perhaps I should become that,' first be still and build a self that is as solid and unmoving as Mount Fuji."

# AUGUST 14

THE GERMAN AUTHOR HERMANN Hesse (1877–1962) writes that the more one matures, the younger one grows. And certainly there are many people who, as they age, become increasingly vigorous and energetic, more broad-minded and tolerant, living with a greater sense of freedom and assurance. It is important to remember that aging and growing old are not necessarily the same thing.

THE FIRST THING IS TO PRAY.
From the moment we begin to pray, things start moving. The darker the night, the closer the dawn. From the moment we chant daimoku with a deep and powerful resolve, the sun begins to rise in our hearts. Hope—prayer is the sun of hope. To chant daimoku each time we face a problem, overcoming it and elevating our life-condition as a result—this is the path of "changing earthly desires into enlightenment," taught in Nichiren Daishonin's Buddhism.

1964: *World Tribune* publishes first issue.

# AUGUST 16

CERTAINLY THERE WILL BE TIMES
when you wish you had more spending
money, more time to sleep and more time for
fun and recreation. You may feel restricted
now, but you should consider your current
situation as the perfect set of circumstances
for your growth. Within the restrictions that
define your present existence, the only thing
to do is to discipline yourself and head in the
direction of growth and self-improvement.
In the process of exerting yourself in such
endeavors, you will without a doubt build and
strengthen your character.

# AUGUST 17

THERE IS NOTHING MORE NOBLE
than inviting our friends to discussion
meetings, gathering together to enable them
to establish a connection with Buddhism, to
talk about Buddhist teachings, and to deepen
our faith. As the Lotus Sutra clearly indicates,
through such steady, dedicated efforts to
teach others about Buddhism, you are
accumulating the good fortune and benefit to
be reborn as great leaders and savor a state of
unsurpassed freedom in lifetime after lifetime.

# AUGUST 18

BUDDHISM IS ACTION.
One meaning of *kyo* of Nam-myoho-renge-kyo
is action. Without action, we cannot say that
we are practicing Nam-myoho-renge-kyo; it
would merely remain a concept. Only
through action are we able to truly gain the
great benefit of the Mystic Law.

# AUGUST 19

BUDDHISM IS WISDOM.
As long as we have wisdom, we can put all things to the best use; we can turn everything in the direction of happiness.

# AUGUST 20

To be fearless no matter what happens—that is the root of true happiness. To move forward resolutely regardless of what lies in store—that is the spirit, the resolve, that leads to human victory. But if we allow ourselves to be disturbed by petty criticism and slander, if we fear pressure and persecution, we will never advance or create anything of lasting value.

# AUGUST 21

THOSE WHO SAY "I'LL DO IT,"
who are willing to take on a challenge even if
they are alone, are true winners. The
determination, the commitment to take
action yourself, is the force that leads to
victory. As Buddhism teaches in the principle
of a life-moment possesses three thousand
realms, our mind or attitude can change
everything.

# AUGUST 22

It is not a question of your environment or those around you, nor what the organization or leaders may be like. To be swayed by such externals is pointless. It all comes down to one person: you. What matters is that you become a brilliant beacon, shining with joy and happiness, and live your life with confidence and courage. If you shine with a radiant light, there can be no darkness in your life.

# AUGUST 23

Shijo Kingo, a person of
strong faith, was at one point envied and
slandered by others, earning the disfavor of
his lord. But later he received a new estate
from him. In modern terms, we might say
that Shijo Kingo scored this victory by
showing wonderful actual proof of faith at
his place of work. The test of faith is winning
in daily life and society, since that is where
Buddhism finds expression.

# AUGUST 24

Advancement—
Nichiren Daishonin teaches the spirit that
"not to advance is to retreat." The point is to
continue forging ahead despite any storms or
hardships that may arise, to be fearless and
advance like a lion.

SGI-USA Men's Division Day
1947: Daisaku Ikeda joins the Soka Gakkai at age 19.

# AUGUST 25

LIFE FLASHES BY IN AN INSTANT. By devoting our lives to Buddhism, we will live a life of complete fulfillment. We are selling ourselves short if we fail to attain such a wonderful state of life.

# AUGUST 26

WE ACCUMULATE GREAT GOOD
fortune through our earnest prayers, devotion
and efforts for the sake of Buddhism,
kosen-rufu and humankind. Prayer without
action is not the way of Nichiren Daishonin's
Buddhism.

# AUGUST 27

THE IMPORTANT THING IS TO KEEP working for kosen-rufu to the very end. On any journey, we cannot hope to reach our destination if we stop halfway. Likewise, if despite our good fortune in meeting and embarking on the unsurpassed way of Buddhism, we stop halfway, all the efforts we have made thus far will have been in vain; we will not be able to attain Buddhahood.

1260: Matsubagayatsu Persecution. Incited by priests, Pure Land believers descend on the Daishonin's hermitage at Matsubagayatsu, Japan, to kill him. He is forced to flee for his life.

# AUGUST 28

SUCCESS IS NOT A MATTER OF accumulating more of this or that; it is not measured in quantity. It means changing the *quality* of your life. Wealth, power, fame and knowledge alone cannot make you happy, no matter how much of these you acquire. Nor can you take them with you when you die. But by improving the quality of your life you will at last approach true happiness.

# AUGUST 29

WORLDLY SUCCESS AND GOOD circumstances based on luck can easily crumble. They are as transient as an illusion. But the state of Buddhahood, once attained, can never be destroyed, not for all eternity. We will enjoy an existence overflowing with good fortune and immense joy in lifetime after lifetime.

# AUGUST 30

THE DAISHONIN STATES, "THE voice does the Buddha's work" (*Gosho Zenshu*, p. 708). To chant the Mystic Law is to praise the Gohonzon. Hearing the sound of our daimoku, the heavenly deities will be set into motion and work to protect us. A weak and unclear voice will not move the heavenly deities. That is why it is important for us to chant daimoku with voices that are clear, strong and brimming with joy.

# AUGUST 31

As long as we pray earnestly and sincerely with all our being, if we have strong and genuine faith, even though results may not be immediately visible, they will definitely manifest without fail in generations of our children and our children's children. I would like all of you to have absolute confidence in this.

# SEPTEMBER

# SEPTEMBER 1

A MOTHER'S BELIEFS HAVE A powerful influence on her children. In the realm of Nichiren Daishonin's Buddhism, too, the children of families where the mother's faith is strong invariably develop into admirable adults.

# SEPTEMBER 2

THE STRONGER THE OPPRESSION from without, the stronger one's determination to summon forth one's inner resources to fight against it—this is the spirit of youth.

# SEPTEMBER 3

TRUE CHARACTER IS FORGED ONLY through hardship and suffering. Moreover, it is the mentor–disciple relationship, not organizational structure, that builds character. Many great scholars, pioneers and leaders of the world have come to note how crucial the mentor–disciple relationship is.

# SEPTEMBER 4

LEADERS WHO ARE RESPONSIBLE for organizing and holding discussion meetings in the SGI must study. If they do not, they cannot hope to satisfy the participants and inspire them with fresh energy and enthusiasm.

# SEPTEMBER 5

YOUNG PEOPLE IN SCHOOL SHOULD make study their first priority. It goes without saying that faith is important, but faith is something we practice throughout our entire lives. There is a certain period and age when we should study. If we don't work hard during that period, we may fail to acquire important knowledge and skills, and we may come to regret it deeply later. Faith manifests itself in daily life. For young people in school, faith manifests itself in their studies. During this period, to devote themselves to study represents an important part of their practice of faith.

# SEPTEMBER 6

We OFTEN HEAR PEOPLE SAY THEY aren't capable. But this is a defeatist attitude. If you feel you aren't capable, then tap into the great reservoir of potential that lies inside you. Since we embrace the Daishonin's Buddhism, we have recourse to daimoku. If we chant daimoku to the Gohonzon, we can bring forth all the ability and strength we will ever need.

# SEPTEMBER 7

FREEDOM DOESN'T MEAN AN
absence of all restrictions. It means possessing
unshakable conviction in the face of any
obstacle. This is true freedom.

# SEPTEMBER 8

WITHOUT OPPOSITION THERE IS no growth. It is hard to argue with that logic. A state in which we are free from problems or constraints is not happiness. Happiness is transcending all opposition and obstacles and continuing to grow.

1957: President Josei Toda makes a declaration against the use of nuclear weapons.

# SEPTEMBER 9

RATHER THAN SITTING AROUND
idly and rusting, we must act, give of
ourselves and contribute something to the
world. The French scholar Robert Arnauld
(1588–1674) declared, "Have we not all
eternity to rest in?" Why do you seek to rest
while you are still alive? he asks. These are
venerable words indeed. When young people
make truly dedicated efforts, almost
punishing themselves, their true brilliance
will shine forth.

YOUTH MEANS TO CHERISH HOPE; it is a time of development. Youth means to challenge oneself; it is a time of construction. Youth means to fight for justice; it is a time of action.

# SEPTEMBER 11

NOTHING CAN MATCH THE
strength of those whose lives have been
shaped and forged through challenging and
overcoming hardships. Such people fear
nothing. The purpose of our Buddhist
practice is to develop such strength and
fortitude. To cultivate such an invincible core
is in itself a victory. It is also the greatest
benefit. Those who can succeed in this
endeavor will savor unsurpassed happiness;
they can manifest the supreme state of
Buddhahood.

# SEPTEMBER 12

I HOPE YOU MEMBERS OF THE
youth division will, in the spirit of Shijo
Kingo, advance with the Daishonin and also
with Mr. Makiguchi, Mr. Toda and myself.
This spirit of joint struggle shared by mentor
and disciple is the very heart of the SGI. It
represents a solidarity in which people are
linked by a true unity of purpose and
commitment. May each one of you lead the
most valuable, meaningful youth. The age
belongs to you.

1271:  Tatsunokuchi Persecution. The Daishonin, who is
       about to be beheaded by government troops, is
       saved when a flash of light in the night sky frightens
       the executioners away. The government later decides
       to exile him to Sado Island.

# SEPTEMBER 13

THE FUNCTIONS OF BOTH THE "devil" and the "Buddha" exist within our lives. Ultimately, our battle is with ourselves. Whether in our Buddhist practice or in activities in society, or whether in historical, political or economic developments, everything essentially boils down to a struggle between positive and negative forces.

# SEPTEMBER 14

ONE'S TRUE WORTH AS A HUMAN being is not a matter of outward appearance or title but derives rather from the breadth of one's spirit. Everything comes down to faith and conviction. It is what is in one's heart and the substance of one's actions that count.

# SEPTEMBER 15

I HOPE THAT EACH OF YOU WILL realize success in your respective fields, fully recognizing that success means not giving up halfway but resolutely pursuing the path you have chosen. To this end, it is also important that you realize that the place where you work is a place for forging your character and growing as a human being. By extension, therefore, it is a place for your Buddhist practice, a place for practicing and deepening your faith. When you view things from this angle, all your complaints will disappear. No one is more pathetic than someone who is constantly complaining.

# SEPTEMBER 16

A NURSE WHO HAS CARED FOR many terminal patients has observed, "Ultimately, people only die as they have lived." To die happily is therefore extremely difficult. And since death is the final settlement of accounts for one's life, it is when our true self comes to the fore. We practice faith to live happily and also to die happily. One who has faith in the Mystic Law will not die an unhappy death.

# SEPTEMBER 17

BUDDHISM TEACHES, THROUGH
the example of Bodhisattva Never
Disparaging, to never look down on anyone.
This is the essence of Buddhism. Nichiren
Daishonin states that the "ultimate
transmission" of Buddhism is to accord
friends and fellow believers who are striving
for kosen-rufu the same respect and reverence
one would a Buddha.

# SEPTEMBER 18

HOW CAN WE CREATE THE
greatest value in the short span of a lifetime?
Those of us who embrace the Mystic Law
know the answer. Our faith in and practice of
the Daishonin's Buddhism enable us in this
lifetime to solidify the world of Buddhahood
in our lives and establish a state of eternal
happiness. That is the purpose of faith in the
Mystic Law, the purpose of our Buddhist
practice.

# SEPTEMBER 19

OUR EXISTENCE IN THIS WORLD can be likened to a dream. The issue of the greatest importance and eternal relevance is how we face death, the inescapable destiny of all living beings. For in the face of death, external factors such as social status or position in the organization count for naught. Everything depends on one's faith, one's state of life.

WHEN YOUR DETERMINATION changes, everything else will begin to move in the direction you desire. The moment you resolve to be victorious, every nerve and fiber in your being will immediately orient itself toward your success. On the other hand, if you think "This is never going to work out," then at that instant every cell in your being will be deflated and give up the fight, and then everything really *will* move in the direction of failure.

IN THE TWINKLING OF AN EYE WE grow old. Our physical strength wanes and we begin to suffer various aches and pains. We practice Nichiren Daishonin's Buddhism so that instead of sinking into feelings of sadness, loneliness and regret, we can greet old age with an inner richness and maturity as round and complete as a ripe, golden fruit of autumn. Faith exists so that we can welcome smiling and without regrets an old age that is like a breathtaking sunset whose dazzling rays color heaven and earth in majestic hues.

# SEPTEMBER 22

THE PRINCIPLE THAT "BUDDHISM equals life" means that everything in one's life is itself Buddhism. The principle that "Buddhism becomes manifest in society" means that society, too, is one with Buddhism. The struggle for kosen-rufu can be waged only within the realities of life and society. Those who earnestly grapple with these realities develop strength and inner substance. They develop and grow.

WINNING IN LIFE IS NOT A MATTER of form or appearances. It has nothing to do with vanity. Victory in life ultimately hinges on whether one has truly fought, whether one has truly advanced.

# SEPTEMBER 24

WHAT KINDS OF CAUSES AM I
making right now?" "What actions am I
taking?" The answers to these questions are
what will determine our future—in this life
and throughout the three existences. Herein
lies the foundation of faith. True glory and
victory in life lie in basing oneself on this
fundamental principle.

1993: The Boston Research Center for the Twenty-first
Century is founded by SGI President Ikeda.

# SEPTEMBER 25

EVERYTHING ULTIMATELY DEPENDS on whether there is someone who is willing to wage a desperate all-out struggle, someone who will take one hundred percent responsibility without relying on or leaving things to others, someone who will work with selfless dedication for the sake of the people without any concern for what others think. Such a person is a true leader and a genuine Buddhist.

# SEPTEMBER 26

OUR VOICE COSTS NOTHING AND it is our strongest weapon. Nichiren Daishonin wrote, "Do not spare your voice" (*Gosho Zenshu*, p. 726). There are different voices for different situations: the clear, resounding voice that declares truth and justice; the strong voice that refutes evil; the bright, confident voice that tells others about the greatness of this Buddhism; the warm voice that gives encouragement; the sincere, friendly voice that offers praise and words of appreciation to others. The important thing is that we meet and speak with people widely, inside and outside the organization.

# SEPTEMBER 27

PIONEERING TAKES STEADY
dedicated effort; it is advancing surely one
step at a time. True Buddhist practice lies in
such activities as visiting members, giving
personal encouragement, talking to our
friends about Buddhism and introducing
others to faith. How many members do you
take the time to visit and encourage in a
month? In a year? True pioneering lies in
making precisely such efforts. Our challenge is
to deepen the understanding of friends
and fellow members toward the philosophy
and activities of the SGI through our
encounters with them.

# SEPTEMBER 28

FAITH MEANS MAKING A HUNDRED percent effort ourselves—in our daimoku and in our actions. When we practice in this way, the Buddhist gods will lend us their protection. We mustn't have a complacent, dependent attitude in faith, chanting haphazardly without definite goals and making only halfhearted efforts in the belief that we'll automatically be protected. Depth of determination and unshakable character are vital. Those possessing these qualities are second to none in faith.

FAITH, WHICH AT FIRST GLANCE
may appear weak, is actually the most
powerful force in the world. Many people put
on a show of being strong, but true strength
has nothing to do with appearances. On the
contrary, we usually find that the weaker
the individual, the greater his or her bravado
or outward display of strength.

THOSE WHO STRENGTHEN THEIR
faith day by day and month after month are
genuine practitioners. Our daily practice of
gongyo, therefore, is important, as well as
attending meetings every month. We must
not let our faith grow weak. We must make it
stronger today than yesterday, stronger this
month than last. Buddhist practice is a
succession of such untiring efforts, the
ultimate goal of which is attaining the summit
of Buddhahood.

# OCTOBER

# OCTOBER 1

I HOPE THAT LEADERS WILL earnestly pray for the prosperity, safety and happiness of the members who are all so infinitely noble and praiseworthy. May you also never forget to develop yourselves and pray to become people who are liked and trusted by the members, who can work unstintingly for the members' happiness and well-being.

# OCTOBER 2

PLEASE MAKE EVERY EFFORT TO find and raise capable people. My wish is that you construct a wonderful organization, joyfully building growing spheres of friendship and a solidarity of people who cherish hope for life and the future. Please lead the most wonderful of lives.

World Peace Day

1960: President Ikeda lands in Hawaii on his first trip outside Japan, beginning his worldwide efforts for peace, culture and education based on Nichiren Daishonin's Buddhism.

# OCTOBER 3

Never be shaken, no matter what happens or what others may say. Never be flustered; never lose confidence. This is the way we should strive to live our lives. Being able to do so is a sign of genuine character.

# OCTOBER 4

WE ARE PEOPLE OF FAITH, AND faith is the ultimate conviction. Nothing could be sadder nor more shortsighted, therefore, than complaining or giving up when we encounter some small obstacle in our path. A genuine Buddhist is a person of wisdom and conviction.

# OCTOBER 5

Nichiren Daishonin said to one of his lay followers: "I entrust you with the propagation of Buddhism in your province. Because the seeds of Buddhahood sprout in response to the proper influence, one expounds the teaching of the one vehicle" (MW-5, 151). Forming connections with other human beings is important. For each of us, everything starts with developing ties with others, forging bonds of friendship and winning trust.

SGI-USA Day

1960: President Ikeda arrives in San Francisco on his first trip to the continental United States, setting in motion the American movement to spread the Daishonin's Buddhism. At Coit Tower, President Ikeda declares that this day will one day be looked upon as a significant step forward for the Daishonin's Buddhism.

Mr. Toda once told me: "You can make a defeat the cause for future victory. You can also make victory the cause for future defeat." The Buddhism of Nichiren Daishonin is the Buddhism of the true cause, the Buddhism of the present and future. We don't dwell on the past. We are always challenging ourselves from the present toward the future. "The whole future lies ahead of us! We have only just begun!"—because we advance with this spirit, we will never be deadlocked.

# OCTOBER 7

WHAT WILL THE FUTURE BE LIKE?
No one knows the answer to that question.
All we know is that the effects that will appear
in the future are all contained in the causes
that are made in the present. The important
thing, therefore, is that we stand up and take
action to achieve great objectives without
allowing ourselves to be distracted or
discouraged by immediate difficulties.

# OCTOBER 8

When you encounter a wall, you should tell yourself, "Since there is a wall here, a wide, open expanse must lie on the other side." Rather than becoming discouraged, know that encountering a wall is proof of the progress that you have made so far. I hope that you will continually advance in your Buddhist practice with this conviction blazing ever more strongly in your heart.

# OCTOBER 9

THERE MAY BE TIMES, CERTAINLY, when being a member of an organization seems bothersome and we just want to be alone. But how sad it is if we are left alone without any support and then lose our faith. True growth comes from striving together with our fellow members in the living realm of human beings, experiencing the rich gamut of human emotions.

# OCTOBER 10

IT DOESN'T MATTER IN WHAT AREA, just keep working on your personal revolution to transform and improve yourself in the way most natural for you. The important thing is that you change in some positive way. There is surely no more exhilarating a life than one in which we write our own unique history of human revolution each day. And the growth and transformation we achieve in this way can convince people of the greatness of the Daishonin's Buddhism more eloquently than anything else.

# OCTOBER 11

It is important to have a sufficiently elevated life-condition so that you will be able to calmly accept whatever happens in life, striving to put problems into proper perspective and solving them with a positive attitude. Happiness blossoms forth from such a strong and all-encompassing life-condition.

# OCTOBER 12

THE GOHONZON ENCOMPASSES THE entire universe. Therefore, we who believe in and chant daimoku to the Gohonzon can live out our lives with the greatest serenity and composure. Please be confident that through faith in the Mystic Law we can definitely lead a wonderful and unsurpassed existence.

1279: Nichiren Daishonin inscribes the Dai-Gohonzon for all humanity.

# OCTOBER 13

ONCE WE HAVE ATTAINED
Buddhahood, we will be Buddhas in lifetime
after lifetime. We will enjoy a state of absolute
freedom throughout eternity. The
Daishonin's golden words say so. This is the
reason we practice faith.

1282: Nichiren Daishonin dies.

# OCTOBER 14

TRUE JOY IS TO BE FOUND IN working for kosen-rufu, in practicing and taking action for the happiness of oneself and others. The greatest joy in life is to be found in SGI activities. Our activities for kosen-rufu become memories that shine ever more brilliantly in our lives as time goes by.

THERE IS NO NEED TO BE
impatient. Anything that is accomplished
quickly and easily will not long endure. Now
is the time to concentrate on the construction
of a solid foundation. I hope you will
complete this work slowly but surely, filled
with hope and joy.

# OCTOBER 16

INTELLECT WILL PLAY A VERY
important role in the coming age. By intellect
I mean refined wisdom, clear reasoning,
profound philosophy and broad-ranging
knowledge. We are entering an age
when people will develop their intelligence
and wisdom, infusing society with their new
outlook.

# OCTOBER 17

I HOPE THAT EACH OF YOU WILL study broadly and develop your understanding of life, society and the universe, based on your faith in Nichiren Daishonin's Buddhism. This type of learning enables you to cultivate a rich state of life, or inner world, drawing forth profound wisdom and limitless leadership ability from the depths of your life.

# OCTOBER 18

A VICTOR IS ONE WHOSE LIFE shines with faith. Emerson, one of the favorite writers of my youth, once said, "That which befits us . . . is cheerfulness and courage, and the endeavor to realize our aspirations." To advance toward our dreams cheerfully, to courageously work toward achieving them— this is what gives sublime meaning and value to our lives.

NO MATTER WHAT HAPPENS, please continue to chant daimoku—in both good times and bad, irrespective of joys or sorrows, happiness or suffering. Then you will be able to seize victory in your daily life and in society.

# OCTOBER 20

Pᴿᴇꜱɪᴅᴇɴᴛ Tᴏᴅᴀ ᴅᴇᴛᴇꜱᴛᴇᴅ
formality. And for this reason, as his disciple,
I have tried to place foremost emphasis on
substance. Formalities are important in certain
cases, but mere formality without substance is
evil. Formalities in and of themselves have no
life, whereas substance is alive. Formality is
provisional and substance essential. Formality
is conventional and therefore conservative,
but substance provides the impetus for
progress and development.

# OCTOBER 21

The mentality of getting others to do the hard work while one sits back and takes it easy—that is bureaucratism at its worst; it is not faith. The spirit of taking on the hard work oneself—that is faith, that is humanism.

THE MAIN POINT IS TO ENABLE one member to stand up by imparting heartfelt assurance and understanding. It is the explosion of faith in the microcosm of an individual that causes the macrocosm of the organization—a gathering of many such individuals—to commence its revolution. This is how the doctrine of a life-moment possesses three thousand realms applies to our practice.

# OCTOBER 23

As far as the fundamental teachings of Buddhism and the Gosho are concerned, I hope that, regarding them as absolutely correct, you will first and foremost strive to put them into practice. I urge you to do so because this is the shortest route to understanding the essence of Buddhism in the depths of your life.

THE ONLY WAY TO SUCCEED IS BY first bringing to completion that which is most immediate. This principle applies in all affairs—in our daily lives, our work and our families as well as in the progress of kosen-rufu.

# OCTOBER 25

It is the sharp sword of the Mystic Law and the great power of faith that enable us to completely sever the chains of suffering. Therefore, I wish to make it clear that to secure eternal freedom and happiness, you must absolutely not be cowardly, especially in faith.

# OCTOBER 26

I HOPE THAT, BASING YOURSELF
on faith, you will become wealthy people of
virtue and influence who are widely respected.
I would like to add, however, that worldly
success is not equivalent to true happiness.
Achieving this requires that we have a
profound understanding of the nature of life.
A person of success in the true sense is
one who can enjoy a free and unrestrained
state of life.

# OCTOBER 27

Whether we regard difficulties in life as misfortunes or whether we view them as good fortune depends entirely on how much we have forged our inner determination. It all depends on our attitude or inner state of life. With a dauntless spirit, we can lead a cheerful and thoroughly enjoyable life. We can develop a "self" of such fortitude that we can look forward to life's trials and tribulations with a sense of profound elation and joy: "Come on obstacles! I've been expecting you! This is the chance that I've been waiting for!"

# OCTOBER 28

It may seem perfectly all right to put ourselves and our own wishes first, to simply follow the dictates of our emotions and cravings, but the truth is that there is nothing more unreliable than our own mind. Life doesn't always go like clockwork and things will not necessarily turn out as we hope or plan. Consequently, Nichiren Daishonin frequently stressed: You should become the master of your mind, not let your mind master you. We mustn't allow ourselves to be ruled by a self-centered mind. Rather, we have to discipline our mind and gain mastery over it. This is the Daishonin's strict admonition.

GONGYO IS A PRACTICE THAT
calls forth and activates the infinite power
that the microcosm inherently possesses. It
transforms your fate, breaks through any
apparent dead ends and converts sufferings
into happiness. It creates a transformation, a
revolution of the microcosm. It is a diagram
in miniature of kosen-rufu in our lives.

# OCTOBER 30

THE GOHONZON IS THE CONCRETE
manifestation of the very existence of
Nichiren Daishonin, who taught kosen-rufu.
Because of that, if you only practice gongyo
and chant daimoku and don't take any other
action for the sake of kosen-rufu or improving
your own life, the Gohonzon will not have its
true, full effect. If, however, you take actions
to achieve kosen-rufu, they will serve as that
extra push for your own life and help you leap
to higher and higher states of mind in your
gongyo and chanting as well.

# OCTOBER 31

It is only natural that sometimes we fall sick. But we must see that sickness as a sickness that originally exists in life, based on the principle of the Mystic Law. In other words, there is no reason to allow yourself to be controlled by illness, for it to fill your life with suffering and distress. From the standpoint of eternal life through the three existences, your fundamentally happy self is incontrovertibly established.

# NOVEMBER

# NOVEMBER 1

THE DAISHONIN HAS TAUGHT US that through gongyo and chanting daimoku we can reach an elevated state in which, while engaged in our daily lives, we travel throughout the entire universe. When you worship the Gohonzon, the door to your microcosm is opened to the entire universe, the macrocosm, and you experience a great, boundless joy, as if you were looking out over the entire cosmos. You feel great satisfaction and rejoicing, a great wisdom, as if you held the entire universe in your palm.

# NOVEMBER 2

THERE ARE CASES WHEN WE
wonder why merit doesn't reveal itself in spite
of our earnest and high degree of faith. At
such times, rather than suspecting that you
may entertain doubt about the Gohonzon, it
is better to ask yourself whether you are guilty
of a type of slander. Because a person who is
contemptuous, hating, jealous or holds
grudges will realize no benefits.

BUDDHISM PLACES THE HIGHEST
value on human rights and seeks to ensure
that human rights are respected. In caring for
just one person, one tries to thoroughly
protect and do everything he can for that
person. One who respects and embraces the
children of the Buddha in this way is a truly
capable person and a true leader.

THE PURPOSE OF FAITH IS TO become happy. I hope all of you will take this sure path to happiness, never wandering onto byroads that lead to unhappiness. Please walk the great path of kosen-rufu with confidence and pride.

# NOVEMBER 5

It is important that we live cheerfully. With a strong spirit of optimism, we need to be able to continually direct our minds in a bright, positive and beneficial direction and help those around us do so, too. We should strive to develop a state of life where we feel a sense of joy no matter what happens.

# NOVEMBER 6

To ESTABLISH MEANINGFUL LIVES, I hope that during your youth you will work hard to polish your intellect. Life, in a sense, is a battle of wisdom. It is the power of Buddhism that enables one to win this battle. True faith is characterized by a brilliance of intellect and depth of wisdom that result from devotion to practice.

# NOVEMBER 7

Throughout his life,
Shakyamuni encouraged people with his clear,
sonorous voice. A Buddhist text describes
how Shakyamuni warmheartedly welcomed
everyone he met, expressing his joy at seeing
them. He showed affection, joy and
gentleness in all his interactions. He greeted
everyone with courtesy and respect. He never
scowled or grimaced. And to put others at
ease and encourage them to speak up,
Shakyamuni would always break the ice by
initiating the conversation. It was the power
of Shakyamuni's eloquence and sincerity that
made it possible for Buddhism to gain wide
acceptance among the people of his time.

# NOVEMBER 8

In the "Record of the Orally
Transmitted Teachings," Nichiren Daishonin
says with reference to attaining Buddhahood,
"'To attain' means 'to open'" (*Gosho Zenshu*,
p. 753). Attaining Buddhahood means
opening our lives to their fullest potential and
revealing our innate Buddhahood. This is
the purpose of Buddhism.

THE DAISHONIN EXPLAINS THE significance of cause and effect: All sutras other than the Lotus Sutra expound that Buddhahood (effect), can be attained only after having made good causes, that is, practicing their teachings (causes), over a length of time. With the Lotus Sutra, however, the very act of embracing it (cause) enables one simultaneously to become a Buddha (effect).

# NOVEMBER 10

THERE ARE VARIOUS KINDS OF
careers and roles that people fill in society.
While each role of course has significance, the
fundamental role that we each play as a
Buddhist is that of philosopher of life and of
humanity who can impart eternal value to
humankind. We are leaders of happiness and
creators of peace. In this sense, our role is
unique.

# NOVEMBER 11

THE TWENTIETH CENTURY WAS A century of war and peace, a century of politics and economics. The dawning twenty-first century holds the promise, however, to be a century of humanity and culture, a century of science and religion. I hope all of you will advance on this wonderful new path of humanism with pride and confidence, as gallant philosophers of action.

1264: Komatsubara Persecution. Nichiren Daishonin is attacked by swordsmen led by the lord of the region. He receives a slash on his forehead and has his left hand broken, but his followers repel the attack, allowing his escape.

# NOVEMBER 12

I HOPE THAT NO MATTER WHAT happens, you will always advance with hope. Especially I hope that the more desperate your circumstances, the more you will press on with unflagging hope. Please keep challenging things with a bright and positive spirit, always taking care at the same time to safeguard your health.

Buddhism aims to make people free in the most profound sense; its purpose is not to restrict or constrain. Doing gongyo is a right, not an obligation. Because Buddhism entails practice, tenacious efforts are required, but these are all for your own sake. If you want to have great benefits or to develop a profound state of life, you should exert yourself accordingly.

# NOVEMBER 14

In a family, if one person is unhappy, then so is the entire family. Therefore, I would like you to sincerely pray for and protect one another so that there are no people who are unfortunate and unhappy, or who abandon their faith, and that every person will become happy. These are the kinds of humanistic bonds among fellow members that give birth to true unity. Coercion or force stemming from power and authority is ineffective at critical moments.

# NOVEMBER 15

PLEASE STEADILY ADVANCE ALONG the fundamental path of "faith manifests itself in daily life," living in the way that best suits you. Just as the sun rises every day, if you persistently advance based on the Mystic Law, the absolute Law of the universe, you will definitely be able to lead a life in which all desires are fulfilled, a life that you cannot now even conceive of. Please be convinced that you are now leading the most certain and valuable life.

WHEN WE SPEAK OF SHOWING
actual proof, it doesn't mean we have to try
to put on a show of being in any way more
knowledgeable or accomplished than we are.
It is my hope that, in the manner that best
suits your situation, you will prove the validity
of this Buddhism by steadily improving in
your daily life and in polishing your character,
as well as in your family, place of work and
community.

# NOVEMBER 17

ONLY IF YOU CHALLENGE YOUR
human revolution in a manner that is true to
yourself will the people around you naturally
begin to trust and respect you. That in itself is
the greatest way of laying the groundwork for
the spread of Nichiren Daishonin's
Buddhism.

THE SOKA GAKKAI'S GOAL IS kosen-rufu—realizing human happiness and world peace by widely spreading the philosophy and ideals of Nichiren Daishonin's Buddhism. We will continue to strive earnestly for this goal, undaunted by criticism, slander or malicious attempts to hinder our progress. That is because what we are doing is the will and decree of the original Buddha, Nichiren Daishonin. I proclaim that all who energetically exert themselves for the cause of kosen-rufu are genuine disciples of the Daishonin and genuine members of the SGI.

Soka Gakkai Founding Day

1930: Soka Gakkai is established.

1944: Tsunesaburo Makiguchi, the Soka Gakkai's first president, dies in prison.

# NOVEMBER 19

THE INNATE POWER OF HUMANITY is the driving force that breaks down all barriers of discrimination. The ultimate expression of this humanity is Buddhahood; it is the power of the Mystic Law. Daimoku is therefore the fundamental energy for realizing victory in the struggle for human rights.

# NOVEMBER 20

WHAT IS THE PURPOSE OF LIFE?
It is happiness. But there are two kinds of
happiness: relative and absolute. Relative
happiness comes in a wide variety of forms.
The purpose of Buddhism is to attain
Buddhahood. In modern terms, this could be
explained as realizing absolute happiness—
a state of happiness that can never be
destroyed or defeated.

# NOVEMBER 21

If you practice faith while doubting its effects, you will get results that are at best unsatisfactory. This is the reflection of your own weak faith on the mirror of the cosmos. On the other hand, when you stand up with strong confidence, you will accrue limitless blessings.

THERE IS A RUSSIAN PROVERB
that says: "It is no use to blame the looking
glass if your face is awry." Likewise, one's
happiness or unhappiness is entirely the
reflection of the balance of good and bad
causes accumulated in one's life. No one can
blame others for his misfortunes. In the world
of faith, it is necessary to realize this all the
more clearly.

IF I WERE TO MAKE AN ANALOGY, thought and philosophy would be like the heart or respiratory system of the human body. When the heart is sound, the whole body can maintain healthy activity. This same principle applies to both the individual and society. The SGI has a mission to serve as the heart that ensures the healthy functioning of society. Consequently, taking good care of the SGI (the heart) allows the fresh life-giving blood of humanism to flow to and nourish all areas of society, including culture, politics and the economy.

# NOVEMBER 24

Rosa Parks wrote in her book *Quiet Strength*: "I find that if I am thinking too much of my own problems and the fact that at times things are not just like I want them to be, I do not make any progress at all. But if I look around and see what I can do, and then I do it, I move on." Youth, and indeed life itself, flashes by in the blink of an eye. That is why it is important for you young people to ask yourselves what you can do for those who are suffering, what you can do to resolve the contradictions that plague society and to boldly take on these great challenges.

Please do not forget your mother's love or the hardships she has endured for you. I am convinced that while people keep the memory of their mothers' loving faces alive in their minds, they will never go far astray. Similarly, as long as we bear in mind the Daishonin's profound compassion and live in deep appreciation of it, our lives will be illuminated brightly by the light of Buddhahood. And enveloped in the Gohonzon's great compassion, we will walk along a path that is filled with tranquillity and immeasurable joy.

BUDDHISM TEACHES THAT BEING led astray by evil friends (negative influences) is to be feared more than being killed by a mad elephant. A mad elephant can only destroy our physical body, but evil friends, if we allow ourselves to be influenced by them, will drag us down into a state of Hell.

# NOVEMBER 27

FAITH IS THE ULTIMATE ESSENCE of intellect. Through the practice of correct faith, the intellect comes to shine. Intellect without correct faith lacks a firm anchor in the soil of life and eventually becomes disordered. This prompted the first Soka Gakkai president, Tsunesaburo Makiguchi, to remark that many modern thinkers were suffering from what he termed "higher psychosis." Faith without intellect, meanwhile, leads to blind faith and fanaticism. Faith or intellect alone—one without the other—is unhealthy.

# NOVEMBER 28

Nᴜᴄʜɪʀᴇɴ Dᴀɪsʜᴏɴɪɴ ᴅɪsᴄᴜssᴇs the meaning of the Chinese characters for the word *benefit* (Jpn *kudoku*) as follows: "The *ku* of *kudoku* means to extinguish evil and *doku* means to bring forth good" (*Gosho Zenshu*, p. 762). We fight against those who try to destroy the True Law. That struggle purifies us and brings forth benefits in our lives. Justice or happiness without a battle is just an illusion. Thinking that happiness means a life free of hard work and effort is fantasy.

Day of Spiritual Independence

1991: Nichiren Shoshu excommunicates twelve million SGI members worldwide.

COMPASSION IS THE VERY SOUL
of Buddhism. To pray for others, making their
problems and anguish our own; to embrace
those who are suffering, becoming their
greatest ally; to continue giving them our
support and encouragement until they
become truly happy—it is in such humanistic
actions that the Daishonin's Buddhism lives
and breathes.

PRESIDENT TODA OFTEN SAID: "Those of you who have problems or sufferings, pray earnestly! Buddhism is a deadly serious win-or-lose struggle. If you should [pray with such an earnest attitude] and still have no solution forthcoming, then I will give you my life!" This invincible conviction on which Mr. Toda was willing to stake his life inspired the members.

# DECEMBER

# DECEMBER 1

Buddhism means putting the
teachings into practice. Practice equals faith.
With sincere prayer and action, our desires
cannot possibly fail to be fulfilled. When you
continue to apply yourselves to your Buddhist
practice toward kosen-rufu, solidifying and
gaining mastery in your faith, you will find
that all your prayers will definitely be
answered.

# DECEMBER 2

NICHIREN DAISHONIN WRITES, "If you light a lantern for another, it will also brighten your own way" (*Gosho Zenshu*, p. 1598). Please be confident that the higher your flame of altruistic action burns, the more its light will suffuse your life with happiness. Those who possess an altruistic spirit are the happiest people of all.

# DECEMBER 3

FAITH IS THE SECRET TO
happiness for all people. When you truly forge
your mind of faith, you will become an eternal
victor throughout the three existences of past,
present and future. Strong faith enables you
to display your wisdom appropriately, so that
you can take advantage of change and move
forward in the direction of victory and hope.

# DECEMBER 4

IN ANY EARNEST STRUGGLE, THERE come crucial challenges—mountains that must be scaled and conquered if we are to win. In Buddhist practice, too, we face such crucial challenges. If we hope to advance kosen-rufu and attain Buddhahood, then we must prevail over these mountains.

# DECEMBER 5

IF YOU PRACTICE FAITH YET HAVE
an attitude of complaint, you will destroy
your good fortune in direct proportion.
Those who are full of complaint are not
respected by others. From both Buddhist and
secular perspectives, their behavior does not
befit a wise or worthy person.

# DECEMBER 6

Where can we find the royal road to reformation and change? Emerson declared: "Not he is great who can alter matter, but he who can alter my state of mind." He strongly urged us to undergo an inner reformation. I want you to be assured that the challenge to which we set ourselves day after day—that of our human revolution—is the royal road to bringing about a reformation in our families, local regions and societies. An inner revolution is the most fundamental and at the same time the ultimate revolution for engendering change in all things.

# DECEMBER 7

It is our hearts that change others' hearts. Friendship changes people. Travelers who pull their capes over their shoulders and brace themselves determinedly against the cold wind naturally relax and change their outlook and actions when warmed by the sun.

# DECEMBER 8

Joy is not simply your personal, egoistic happiness. Nor is it making others happy at the expense of your own happiness. You and others delighting together, you and others becoming happy together—this is the Mystic Law and the wondrous thing about our realm of kosen-rufu. The Daishonin states, "Joy means that both oneself and others have wisdom and compassion" (*Gosho Zenshu*, p. 761).

# DECEMBER 9

Faith means infinite hope, and infinite hope resides in the SGI. As long as your faith is sincere, infinite glory, boundless good fortune and endless victory will unfold before you. You will never find yourselves at a dead end.

# DECEMBER 10

We must put down firm roots; we must be strong. Inner strength is a prerequisite for happiness, a prerequisite for upholding justice and one's beliefs. One of the Buddha's titles is "He Who Can Forbear." To courageously endure, persevere and overcome all difficulties—the Buddha is the ultimate embodiment of the virtue of forbearance. The power of faith gives us the strength to weather and survive any storm. Perseverance is the essence of a Buddha.

# DECEMBER 11

Pᴿᴱˢᴵᴰᴱᴺᵀ Tᴏᴅᴀ ᴜˢᴇᴅ ᴛᴏ ˢᴀʏ, "Become individuals who are strong physically, intellectually and spiritually." To be strong in all three areas is the ideal. Many people may be strong in one or two of these areas, but only when all three are combined can we enjoy a well-balanced life, a life of resounding victory. Those who cultivate such all-around strength are never defeated.

# DECEMBER 12

SOMETIMES YOUR CHILDREN MAY not be able to do gongyo, but there is no reason for parents to become overly concerned or agitated about this. There are times when chanting only three daimoku is sufficient. To continue practicing [even though gongyo may not be consistent] is far more important. What matters is that the children maintain their connection to the Gohonzon and the SGI for their entire lives.

# DECEMBER 13

THE ORGANIZATION OF FAITH IS
not something that holds you back or restricts
you. Rather, it is a springboard that enables
you to develop yourself to the utmost and to
lead the most dynamic existence. It is the
most precious place for carrying out our
Buddhist practice.

# DECEMBER 14

Faith MANIFESTS ITSELF AS wisdom. The purpose of our faith is to become wise, so that we can live wisely. The desire to save others becomes merely an abstract goal if those who practice faith cannot communicate with their own children nor build strong and happy families.

# DECEMBER 15

THE GOOD FORTUNE THAT accrues to parents who apply themselves diligently to SGI activities will protect their children without fail. Based on this conviction, you must still make positive efforts to open and sustain dialogue with your children, not allowing yourselves to neglect them, claiming that you're too busy or it can't be helped, or telling yourselves that somehow things will be taken care of. Unless you exert yourselves in this way, you are irresponsible parents who lack compassion.

# DECEMBER 16

OUTWARD APPEARANCE IS NOT important—what counts is what is inside our hearts. Are there heart-to-heart bonds? Some families may always be together physically but are estranged at heart. Some families can only get together for brief periods but manage to enjoy concentrated and lively heart-to-heart communication when they do meet. Families that share bonds of closeness based on day-to-day efforts are ones in which the members feel comfortable and at ease with one another, no matter where they are or what they're doing.

# DECEMBER 17

WE ARE ALL HUMAN BEINGS;
in that regard, we are all the same. The only
real difference lies in people's life-conditions.
Our life-condition continues beyond death
into eternity. Therefore, as the Daishonin
says, "Faith alone is what really matters."

W<small>E</small> **SGI** <small>MEMBERS</small> <small>DEVOTE</small>
ourselves to serving the Law, serving
humanity. Ours is not an egocentric life. That
is why we are busier than others and perhaps
don't have as much opportunity for relaxation
with our families. Nevertheless, we continue
to devote ourselves to others. Ours is the
most noble way of life. We must make sure
our children can understand and respect our
beliefs, our way of life and our dedication. We
must make conscious efforts to verbalize and
communicate our thoughts and feelings to
them. Finding the wisdom for this task is an
expression of our faith.

# DECEMBER 19

Encouragement—
offering encouraging words—is important.
Nichiren Daishonin states, "The voice does
the Buddha's work" (*Gosho Zenshu*, p. 708).
Sincere words of encouragement have the
power to give people hope and courage to go
on living.

# DECEMBER 20

Pʀᴇsɪᴅᴇɴᴛ Tᴏᴅᴀ ᴜsᴇᴅ ᴛᴏ sᴀʏ:
"Don't be impatient. Since you have
embraced the Gohonzon, your situation will
definitely improve. There's no need to worry.
Sure there will be hard times, times when you
feel like crying. But as long as you have the
Gohonzon, your life will become bright and
joyful." As long as we persevere in faith, we
will become happy. We must never doubt this
no matter what happens but always advance
resolutely, staunchly enduring all hardships
and obstacles along the way. This is what true
faith is.

# DECEMBER 21

Buddhism holds that
everything is in a constant state of flux. Thus
the question is whether we are to accept
change passively and be swept away by it or
whether we are to take the lead and create
positive changes on our own initiative. While
conservatism and self-protection might be
likened to winter, night and death, the spirit
of pioneering and attempting to realize ideals
evokes images of spring, morning and birth.

# DECEMBER 22

Our lives are infinitely precious. To not attain a state of absolute happiness in this lifetime is a great loss. Our Buddhist practice exists so that we can attain indestructible happiness. We must fight to the fullest right now, not sometime in the future.

# DECEMBER 23

Leo Tolstoy concluded that the only way to bring about a fundamental change in society is to realize a change in public opinion, a change in people's minds. Then how can we change public opinion? Tolstoy asserted: "It is only necessary for people to say what they really think or at least to refrain from saying what they do not think." It is vital, in other words, not to be swayed by others' opinions or past ways of thinking or doing. Instead each of us must become wise, possessing our own firm convictions.

# DECEMBER 24

Many religions have demanded blind faith, taking away people's independence. President Makiguchi opposed such enslavement. What he called for instead was solidarity of awakened common people. To achieve this, he proposed a self-reliant way of life in which we advance on the path of our choice with a firm, independent character. He also stressed a contributive way of life in which we set our fundamental goal in life toward the realization of happiness for ourselves and others, casting aside arrogance and self-satisfaction to respect and benefit others.

IF A PERSON IS HUNGRY, WE
should give them bread. When there is no
bread, we can at least give words that nourish.
To a person who looks ill or is physically frail,
we can turn the conversation to some subject
that will lift their spirits and fill them with the
hope and determination to get better. Let us
give something to each person we meet: joy,
courage, hope, assurance, philosophy,
wisdom, a vision for the future. Let us always
give something.

# DECEMBER 26

GOOD HEALTH EQUALS BUDDHISM. Daily life equals faith. Taking care to avoid traffic accidents and making efforts to stay in good health, therefore, are all part of our Buddhist practice. It is important that we live wisely, striving with the awareness each day that all the actions and activities we undertake for the sake of faith contribute to our good health and well-being.

# DECEMBER 27

No MATTER WHAT THE circumstances, you should never concede defeat. Never conclude that you've reached a dead end, that everything is finished. You possess a glorious future. And precisely because of that, you must persevere and study. Life is eternal. We need to focus on the two existences of the present and the future and not get caught up in the past. We must always have the spirit to begin anew "from this moment," to initiate a new struggle each day.

# DECEMBER 28

Kosen-rufu is a very long struggle. It is a march that will continue over the ten thousand years of the Latter Day of the Law. Therefore, let us advance joyfully and unhurriedly. Activities must not be conducted in such a way that people suffer and become exhausted. Meetings should be short and not too numerous and conducted so that they are valuable and productive for all concerned.

WHO IS TRULY GREAT? I HOPE YOU can develop the ability to discern true human greatness. A great person is someone who forges unity among human beings through sincere dialogue, armed with a solid philosophy, feet firmly planted on the ground. A great person is one who lives among the people and earns their unshakable trust. Fickle popularity and temporary fads are nothing but illusions.

# DECEMBER 30

Taking good care of our health is most important. In particular, it is vital for those who are advanced in years to get sufficient rest to avoid becoming fatigued. Sleep is the best medicine. I also hope you will put your wisdom to work and find various ways to improve and maintain your health.

# DECEMBER 31

To LEAD A LIFE IN WHICH WE ARE inspired and can inspire others, our hearts have to be alive; they have to be filled with passion and enthusiasm. To achieve that, as President Toda also said, we need the courage to "live true to ourselves." And to live true to ourselves, we need the strength of mind not to be swayed by our environment or be obsessed with vanity and superficial appearances. Rather than borrowing from or imitating others, we need the conviction to be able to think for ourselves and to take action from our own sense of responsibility.

# CHAPTER 3

# APPENDIX

*All excerpts in this book come from addresses Mr. Ikeda delivered in the 1990s to SGI members around the world. This listing shows the date of the addresses from which each excerpt was taken.*

| | | | |
|---|---|---|---|
| 6/12 · 1/6/96 | 8/2 · 3/20/96 | 9/23 · 10/25/96 | 11/13 · 2/25/90 |
| 6/13 · 1/6/96 | 8/3 · 4/2/96 | 9/24 · 10/25/96 | 11/14 · 2/25/90 |
| 6/14 · 1/6/96 | 8/4 · 4/2/96 | 9/25 · 10/25/96 | 11/15 · 2/26/90 |
| 6/15 · 1/6/96 | 8/5 · 4/2/96 | 9/26 · 11/17/96 | 11/16 · 2/26/90 |
| 6/16 · 3/18/98 | 8/6 · 4/2/96 | 9/27 · 11/23/96 | 11/17 · 2/26/90 |
| 6/17 · 1/6/96 | 8/7 · 2/3/98 | 9/28 · 11/23/96 | 11/18 · 4/20/98 |
| 6/18 · 1/7/96 | 8/8 · 4/2/96 | 9/29 · 5/26/98 | 11/19 · 1/6/96 |
| 6/19 · 1/14/96 | 8/9 · 5/3/96 | 9/30 · 3/24/97 | 11/20 · 2/27/90 |
| 6/20 · 3/20/96 | 8/10 · 5/3/96 | | 11/21 · 2/27/90 |
| 6/21 · 1/26/96 | 8/11 · 3/24/97 | 10/1 · 11/23/96 | 11/22 · 2/27/90 |
| 6/22 · 1/26/96 | 8/12 · 5/3/96 | 10/2 · 7/3/96 | 11/23 · 1/28/93 |
| 6/23 · 1/26/96 | 8/13 · 4/17/96 | 10/3 · 12/16/96 | 11/24 · 4/2/96 |
| 6/24 · 1/26/96 | 8/14 · 1/8/98 | 10/4 · 12/16/96 | 11/25 · 2/22/90 |
| 6/25 · 1/27/96 | 8/15 · 6/15/96 | 10/5 · 6/15/96 | 11/26 · 1/26/96 |
| 6/26 · 1/27/96 | 8/16 · 4/17/96 | 10/6 · 12/16/96 | 11/27 · 1/28/93 |
| 6/27 · 1/27/96 | 8/17 · 4/23/96 | 10/7 · 5/17/97 | 11/28 · 6/5/96 |
| 6/28 · 1/27/96 | 8/18 · 4/23/96 | 10/8 · 3/28/95 | 11/29 · 1/27/93 |
| 6/29 · 3/8/96 | 8/19 · 4/23/96 | 10/9 · 12/16/96 | 11/30 · 1/27/93 |
| 6/30 · 3/8/96 | 8/20 · 4/23/96 | 10/10 · 12/16/96 | |
| | 8/21 · 1/8/98 | 10/11 · 2/12/90 | 12/1 · 1/27/93 |
| 7/1 · 6/9/96 | 8/22 · 4/23/96 | 10/12 · 4/21/98 | 12/2 · 1/31/93 |
| 7/2 · 3/8/96 | 8/23 · 4/23/96 | 10/13 · 1/6/96 | 12/3 · 1/31/93 |
| 7/3 · 5/24/96 | 8/24 · 10/25/96 | 10/14 · 7/9/97 | 12/4 · 1/27/96 |
| 7/4 · 2/14/90 | 8/25 · 5/16/96 | 10/15 · 2/13/90 | 12/5 · 1/31/93 |
| 7/5 · 3/8/96 | 8/26 · 5/24/96 | 10/16 · 2/13/90 | 12/6 · 2/5/93 |
| 7/6 · 3/8/96 | 8/27 · 5/24/96 | 10/17 · 2/14/90 | 12/7 · 2/5/93 |
| 7/7 · 3/8/96 | 8/28 · 3/5/97 | 10/18 · 5/26/98 | 12/8 · 2/5/93 |
| 7/8 · 6/5/96 | 8/29 · 5/23/96 | 10/19 · 2/14/90 | 12/9 · 2/5/93 |
| 7/9 · 2/24/96 | 8/30 · 5/23/96 | 10/20 · 2/15/90 | 12/10 · 2/2/93 |
| 7/10 · 2/24/96 | 8/31 · 5/23/96 | 10/21 · 8/27/97 | 12/1 · 2/2/93 |
| 7/11 · 7/3/96 | | 10/22 · 2/15/90 | 12/12 · 2/3/93 |
| 7/12 · 2/24/96 | 9/1 · 7/19/96 | 10/23 · 2/15/90 | 12/13 · 5/5/97 |
| 7/13 · 3/9/96 | 9/2 · 7/19/96 | 10/24 · 2/17/90 | 12/14 · 2/3/93 |
| 7/14 · 3/9/96 | 9/3 · 7/19/96 | 10/25 · 2/17/90 | 12/15 · 2/3/93 |
| 7/15 · 10/25/96 | 9/4 · 7/19/96 | 10/26 · 2/18/90 | 12/16 · 2/3/93 |
| 7/16 · 5/8/98 | 9/5 · 2/3/93 | 10/27 · 5/21/95 | 12/17 · 9/26/96 |
| 7/17 · 3/17/96 | 9/6 · 6/19/96 | 10/28 · 8/27/97 | 12/18 · 2/3/93 |
| 7/18 · 3/17/96 | 9/7 · 6/19/96 | 10/29 · 2/19/90 | 12/19 · 1/27/95 |
| 7/19 · 5/26/98 | 9/8 · 6/19/96 | 10/30 · 2/19/90 | 12/20 · 1/31/95 |
| 7/20 · 3/29/96 | 9/9 · 6/19/96 | 10/31 · 2/20/90 | 12/21 · 2/21/90 |
| 7/21 · 3/29/96 | 9/10 · 8/18/96 | | 12/22 · 1/31/95 |
| 7/22 · 3/29/96 | 9/11 · 8/29/96 | 11/1 · 2/20/90 | 12/23 · 1/30/95 |
| 7/23 · 6/15/96 | 9/12 · 5/3/96 | 11/2 · 2/20/90 | 12/24 · 1/30/95 |
| 7/24 · 3/18/96 | 9/13 · 3/24/97 | 11/3 · 2/21/90 | 12/25 · 12/16/96 |
| 7/25 · 3/18/96 | 9/14 · 8/29/96 | 11/4 · 1/30/95 | 12/26 · 6/28/95 |
| 7/26 · 4/13/96 | 9/15 · 2/3/93 | 11/5 · 9/15/97 | 12/27 · 4/2/95 |
| 7/27 · 4/13/96 | 9/16 · 9/26/96 | 11/6 · 2/22/90 | 12/28 · 4/11/95 |
| 7/28 · 3/21/96 | 9/17 · 9/26/96 | 11/7 · 1/27/95 | 12/29 · 4/11/95 |
| 7/29 · 4/22/96 | 9/18 · 9/26/96 | 11/8 · 1/28/93 | 12/30 · 5/17/95 |
| 7/30 · 2/21/98 | 9/19 · 9/26/96 | 11/9 · 2/24/90 | 12/31 · 5/18/95 |
| 7/31 · 1/26/96 | 9/20 · 3/24/97 | 11/10 · 2/25/90 | |
| | 9/21 · 6/15/96 | 11/11 · 4/2/98 | |
| 8/1 · 3/20/96 | 9/22 · 10/25/96 | 11/12 · 1/6/96 | |

# INDEX